LOUISIANA

ART OF THE STATE

ART OF THE STATE

LOUISIANA

The Spirit of America

Text by Nancy Friedman

Harry N. Abrams, Inc., Publishers

NEW YORK

This book was prepared for publication at
Walking Stick Press, San Francisco

Project staff:
    Series Designer: Linda Herman
    Series Editor: Diana Landau

For Harry N. Abrams, Inc.:
    Series Editor: Ruth A. Peltason

Page 1: *Washboard Player* by Francis Pavy, 1995. *Arthur Roger Gallery*

Page 2: *Cypress Point, Bayou Lacombe, Louisiana* by Charles Wellington Boyd, 1903.
    The Ogden Museum of Southern Art, University of New Orleans

Library of Congress Cataloguing-in-Publication Data

Friedman, Nancy.
    Louisiana : the spirit of America, state by state / text by Nancy Friedman
       p.   cm. — (Art of the state)
    Includes bibliographical references and index.
    ISBN 0–8109–5554–7 (hardcover)
    1. Louisiana—Miscellanea.   I. Title.   II. Series.
F369.F75   1998
976.3—dc21   98–3991

Harry N. Abrams, Inc.
100 Fifth Avenue
New York, N.Y. 10011
www.abramsbooks.com

The End of an Era by Clarence John Laughlin, 1938. *Historic New Orleans Collection*

"Once French, once Spanish, but now forever American."

Historian Alcée Fortier, 1904

President James Madison surely never heard of "multicultural diversity," but in choosing Louisiana as the first state west of the Mississippi he contributed greatly to it, adding strange and complex flavors to the American melting pot. For Louisiana was utterly unlike its predecessors down the aisle to statehood. Its heritage was French and Spanish, not British; its primary language remained French for decades following statehood in 1812. It was settled not by Protestant refugees or hardy frontiersmen but by Catholic aristocrats and gentry. Even its statutes followed the Napoleonic civil code rather than British common law: trial by jury was a distinct curiosity. Louisiana was an exotic bloom in the American garden, and a somewhat less than willing convert to the American Dream.

Nearly 200 years after statehood, Louisiana still takes enthusiastic pride in its differentness. Make no mistake: Louisiana looks, sounds, smells, and tastes like no other state. From the Caribbean-influenced "shotgun houses" of New Orleans to the French vocabulary casually injected into conversation, from eerie above-ground cemeteries to exuberant Mardi Gras parades, from foot-tapping zydeco to palate-searing gumbo, Louisiana can beguile a visitor into believing he or she has slipped past an invisible boundary into a country that isn't quite the United States. Or even quite the South—certainly not the old-line Anglo-Saxon Protestant South. Although it was a slave state and member of

Café Tupinamba by Caroline Durieux, 1934. *Louisiana State University Museum of Art, Baton Rouge*

the Confederacy, Louisiana was unique in having a large class of "free people of color"—many of whom owned slaves themselves—and, thanks to widespread intermarriage, a complicated, many-tiered system of racial classification.

That said, it can't be denied that some aspects of Louisiana are both familiar and quintessentially American. Travel the rich, rolling prairies of the north state, with their rice fields and cattle ranches, and you might as well be in the heart of the West. Duck into Preservation Hall in New Orleans for some traditional jazz, and you're enjoying the one truly original American music. Cruise the Mississippi River, which forms Louisiana's eastern border, and you're in Mark Twain territory, mingling with riverboats and oil tankers on the great current of American commerce, legend, and history.

And for all its uniqueness, Louisiana is integrally bound up in American culture. "Dixie," a synonym for the South since the Civil War era, had its origins here, in the "dix" note—French for $10—minted in New Orleans. One of the most influential (and unmistakably American) figures of contemporary political history, Huey Long, was born here, elected here, and assassinated here; his radical populist "Share the Wealth" philosophy attracted a national following. And rock 'n' roll would unquestionably have been the poorer without its great Louisiana exponents, from Fats Domino to Jerry Lee Lewis to the Neville Brothers.

Louisiana is as primeval as the alligators in its bayous, as ancient as the mysterious earthen mounds built 4,000 years ago by Native people, as modern as oil rigs in the Gulf of Mexico. It's as sophisticated as dinner at Antoine's and as impudent as a drive-through daiquiri stand. It's as haunting as a tale told by Lafcadio Hearn or Anne Rice, and as dynamic as a soaring Clyde Connell sculpture or a vibrant John McCrady canvas.

Louisiana honors its past to a degree unrecognized in most other American states. A sense of melancholy, of gazing wistfully backward to a lost golden era, pervades much of Louisiana art, from funereal bayou landscapes to the disaffected, quirky protagonists of John Kennedy Toole or Walker Percy. Yet, characteristically in this most contradictory of states, Louisiana also embodies a thoroughgoing enjoyment of the here-and-now best expressed in the Cajun rallying cry, *"Laissez les bon temps rouler!"*—let the good times roll.

The spirit of Louisiana is the spirit of its people, a potpourri of ethnicities and colors. In Cajun country you'll find dark-skinned Moutons and pale-skinned Moutons, all of whom share a 17th-century ancestor named Mouton who left Brittany for Nova Scotia and then fled to Louisiana. In New Orleans you'll hear accented English that sounds half Southern, half Brooklyn, the result of a blended chorus of Irish, Italian, French, and Appalachian voices. Louisiana boasts significant communities of Yugoslavs, Germans, and people whose forebears immigrated from Saint-Domingue and the Canary Islands. Together with the descendants of West African slaves, Choctaw and Chitimacha Indians, French and Spanish sugar planters, they form a remarkable cultural jambalaya that could have been created nowhere else on earth. ❧

New Orleans Chamber of Commerce Chair, 1867. The solid oak chair is carved with Louisiana's state symbols. *Louisiana State Museum*

"Union, Justice

LOUISIANA

"Bayou State"
"Pelican State"
18th State

Date of Statehood
APRIL 30, 1812

Capital
BATON ROUGE

Bird
EASTERN BROWN PELICAN

Flower
MAGNOLIA

Tree
BALD CYPRESS

Gemstone
AGATE

Dog
LOUISIANA CATAHOULA DOG

Crustacean
CRAWFISH

Reptile
ALLIGATOR

History, nature, and personality play equal roles in Louisiana's official symbols.

The state colors bow to colonial France (the gold and white of the royal standard) while standing proud for autonomy (the blue of a briefly independent Louisiana's "Bonnie Blue" flag). The lovely, fragrant magnolia places Louisiana squarely within the generic South, while the bald cypress—a long-lived, moss-draped denizen of the otherworldly bayous—speaks hauntingly of more ancient and local surroundings. The brown pelican, a Gulf Coast native, was admired by Louisiana's first territorial governor, William C. C. Claiborne, for its apparent altruism: it seems to tear at its own flesh rather than let its young starve. And a

Brown pelican and magnolia

later governor, Jimmie H. Davis, wrote "You Are My Sunshine," which, despite making no mention of Louisiana at all, became an official state song in 1977.

Sequoia of the South

Early French explorers were amazed by Louisiana's abundant stands of bald cypress (*Taxodium distichum*), an ancient native related to California's giant sequoias. More amazing still, cypress wood proved extremely hardy, easy to saw and split, and nearly impossible to burn. So useful was this "wood eternal" that by the 19th century much of the state was deforested.

Above: Spirit of Louisiana by George David Coulon, 1884. Born in France, Coulon came to Louisiana as a child and enjoyed a long career as a painter of landscapes, still lifes, and animal studies, as well as of this allegorical portrait. New Orleans Museum of Art Below: The American alligator. Right: Bald cypress.

Gumbo

From the African word for okra, *guingombo*, or from the Choctaw word for sassafras, *kombo*, this flavorful stew is thickened with okra or ground sassafras—filé powder.

Roux (see below)
1 medium onion, chopped
2 stalks celery, chopped
1 clove garlic (or more)
½ green pepper, chopped
About 2 quarts water
1 chicken, quartered
1 pound okra
  or 3 tbsp. filé powder
1 tsp. thyme
1 tsp. Tabasco
1 bay leaf
Optional:
4 oz. andouille sausage
2 large fresh tomatoes

Prepare a roux: melt ¼ lb. butter or margarine, or use ½ cup oil or drippings. Add an equal amount of flour, mix well, turn up heat, and stir constantly for at least 45 minutes. Sauté onion, celery, garlic, and pepper in oil. Combine with roux, add 1 cup water, chicken, okra, spices, and optionals. If substituting filé powder for okra, add it now. Bring to boil. Simmer at least 1 hour; add water as needed. Adjust seasoning; serve over rice.

A Louisiana Glossary

Banquette (BANK-it) Sidewalk (originally wooden and elevated)

Bayou From the Choctaw "bayuk," a sluggish river or natural canal

Beignet (bin-YAY) Hot, hole-less doughnut

Bousillage (boo-see-YAHJ) Mixture of mud and moss used in building

Chênière Low oak-covered ridge beside a river (from French *chêne*, oak)

Etouffée Smothered, as in crawfish étouffée

The state capitol in Baton Rouge. *Photo James Schwabel*

Fais-do-do A country dance (from baby French, "fais dormir": go to sleep)

Garçonnière Bachelor quarters, separate from a main house

Lagniappe (la-NYAHP) "A little extra something" for good measure; from Spanish "la ñapa"

Muffuletta Thick Italian sandwich invented at New Orleans's Central Grocery

Parish County

Pirogue Dugout canoe used in bayous

Po' Boy Foot-long sandwich made with French bread, meats, and gravy

A Zydeco musician with "squeeze box." Zydeco combines traditional Cajun instruments and melodies with African rhythms. *Photo Bonnie Kamin*

Louisiana Catahoula Dog

The state's dog has bloodlines as complex as its people. Its "war dog" ancestors (probably mastiffs or greyhounds) came to Louisiana with Spanish explorer Hernando de Soto in the mid-1600s; left behind with local Catahoula Indians, they mated with red wolves. The modern breed evolved a century later, the result of interbreeding with French Beaucerons. Muscular, web-footed, and often spotted (hence its other name, Catahoula leopard dog), this spirited animal is equally at home in brush or bayou.

"Give Me Louisiana"

Give me Louisiana,
The State where I was born
The State of snowy cotton,
The best I've ever known;
A State of sweet magnolias,
And Creole melodies.

Oh give me Louisiana,
The State where I was born
Oh what sweet old mem'ries
The mossy old oaks bring.
It brings us the story
Of our Evangeline.

A State of old tradition,
Of old plantation days
Makes good ole Louisiana
The sweetest of all States.

*Words and music
by Doralice Fontane*

Top: **Catahoula dog pup.** *Above:* **The state crustacean, known as crawfish, crayfish, *écrevisse,* or mudbug, is served in everything from gumbo to jambalaya to crawfish étouffée.** *Photo Tom McHugh. Right:* **Beignets (the state doughnut) and chicory-flavored coffee.** *Photo Mike Yamashita*

c. 2000–600 B.C. Poverty Point culture flourishes.

1542 Hernando de Soto becomes the first European to enter Louisiana.

1682 La Salle explores the Mississippi to the Gulf of Mexico; he claims the territory for France and names it "Louisiana" after King Louis XIV.

1699 First French settlement in Louisiana, built by Pierre le Moyne, Sieur d'Iberville, at Biloxi Bay.

1755 Some 2,000 French Acadian settlers leave Canada and make their way to Louisiana, where they are known as "Cajuns."

1762 France turns over the unprofitable Louisiana territory to Spain.

1776 Revolutionary War. New Orleans is used as a base to pillage Loyalists in West Florida.

1792 First theater opens in New Orleans.

1714 Establishment of Natchitoches.

1717 Company of the West receives the Louisiana concession. Beginnings of the "Mississippi Bubble" land boom.

1718 New Orleans founded by Jean Baptiste le Moyne, Sieur de Bienville, and named for Philippe, Duc d'Orleans.

1721 New Orleans population is 470 Europeans and about 300 African slaves.

1722 Capital of Louisiana territory moves from Biloxi to New Orleans.

1724 Code Noir (Black Code) enacted; slavery is regulated and Jews are expelled from the territory.

1731 Louisiana becomes a crown colony of France.

1794 The first issue of *Moniteur de la Louisiana,* the state's first newspaper, is published.

1800 Via secret treaty, Louisiana is returned to France.

1803 Napoleon sells the entire Louisiana territory to the U.S. for $15 million. New Orleans population is 4,000 whites, 2,700 black slaves, and 1,300 free people of color.

1812 Louisiana admitted to the Union as 18th state.

1815 New Orleans successfully defended against the British by Colonel Andrew Jackson's troops in the Battle of New Orleans.

1821 John J. Audubon, pioneering painter of bird life, sets up a studio in New Orleans.

1830 State population 215,739.

1840 New Orleans has five theaters and a population of 102,000; it is the fourth-largest city in the U.S. State population is 352,411.

1857 The Mistick Krewe of Comus makes its debut at Mardi Gras.

1859 French Opera House opens in New Orleans.

1860 Population has tripled in 20 years, to 708,002.

1861 Louisiana joins the Confederacy; Civil War begins.

1862 New Orleans falls to Union forces led by Admiral David Farragut.

1868 Louisiana readmitted to Union; black suffrage granted. Reconstruction begins.

1870 The *Robert E. Lee* and the *Natchez*, two great steamboats, begin their historic race at New Orleans. Population 726,915.

1873 Painter Edgar Degas visits his uncle and brothers in New Orleans.

1883 William Woodward comes to Tulane University to teach art; his brother Ellsworth follows.

1890 Pioneering jazz musician Buddy Bolden forms his own band in New Orleans.

1900 Population 1,381,625.

1901 Oil discovered near Jennings.

1905 Last yellow fever epidemic. Louisiana celebrates tricentennial of French arrival.

1910 Isaac Delgado donates $150,000 to New Orleans to build a museum in City Park.

1920 Population 1,798,509.

1928 Huey P. Long elected governor on a "Share the Wealth" platform.

1930 Population 2,101,593.

1934 First issue of *Southern Review* published.

1935 Huey Long is assassinated.

1963 Blacks enter four previously all-white schools in Baton Rouge—the state's first high school integration.

1965 Hurricane Betsy strikes southeastern Louisiana, killing 81 people.

1969 First New Orleans Jazz & Heritage Festival in Congo Square.

1975 Louisiana Superdome completed.

1984 World Exposition held on New Orleans wharves.

1990 Population 4,219,973.

1991 Riverboat gambling legalized in the state. Legislation passed to integrate the Mardi Gras krewes.

Bayou Plaquemines by Joseph R. Meeker, 1881. *Ogden Museum of Southern Art*

Low-lying, semitropical Louisiana has more wetlands than any other state, and parts of it lie far enough below sea level to blur the distinction between land and water. Its largest city, New Orleans, sits a perilous 8 feet below sea level; the highest point, Mount Driskill in northwestern Louisiana, is a modest 535 feet above sea level. Millions of years ago, most of the state lay beneath the waters of the Gulf of Mexico. This maritime past is revealed today in many inland lakes (actually tidal bays), swamps, "land islands," salt domes, and a rich alluvial soil built up over millennia by innumerable floods and ebbs, as the Mississippi River endlessly reshaped its delta.

Despite its overall flatness and wetness, Louisiana's natural diversity is remarkable. Some 150 species of trees thrive here; a small difference in elevation makes a big difference in soil. The northern and western parts of the state comprise pine forest, prairie, rolling hills, and steep bluffs as high as 300 feet. In the south, coastal marshlands extend up to 20 miles inland, separated from the Gulf by low ridges called chênières, after the live oaks (*chênes* in French) that grow on them. ❦

Louisiana is the southern terminus of the Central and Mississippi Flyways; more than half of all North American bird species can be spotted here at some time during the year, from laughing gull and royal tern to blue heron, American egret, and possibly the last ivory-billed woodpecker, living somewhere in the Atchafalaya Basin. *Below: Long-billed Curlew or Corbigeau by Achille Perelli, c. 1880s. Louisiana State Museum*

"…THE PRODIGIOUS GROWTH OF timber, luxuriance of cane, tangle of vines and creepers, astonishing size of the weeds and the strength of vegetation in general."

The Rev. Timothy Flint, visiting in 1818

Down on the Bayou

Below: Flowers and cypress trees in a swamp near Natchitoches. *Below right:* The Atchafalaya Delta. *Photos Philip Gould/ Corbis*

Some 3,500 square miles of Louisiana's land area is actually water. The Mississippi defines the state's eastern border, but many other rivers shape this land. Especially in the Mississippi Delta, rivers fan out into a complex network of bayous, which move in mysterious ways, sometimes obeying the Gulf tides, other times changing direction seemingly at whim. Some are more than 100 miles long and bear legendary names: Bayou Lafourche, the "main street" of Acadiana's Lafourche Parish; Bayou Teche, in the heart of plantation country; Bayou Barataria, the hideout of the infamous 19th-century pirate Jean Lafitte. Smaller bayous go unnamed, or have playful monikers such as Go to Hell, Funny Louis, and Mouchoir de l'Ourse (Bear's Handkerchief). The bayous nurture a wealth of plant and animal life, and continue to inspire artists and writers with their eerie beauty.

"IT IS A PLACE THAT SEEMS OFTEN UNABLE TO MAKE UP ITS MIND whether it will be earth or water, and so it compromises."

Harnett T. Kane, The Bayous of Louisiana, *1943*

"ALL ALONG THIS NORTHERN EDGE OF THE GULF THERE IS ALMOST no solid land, just the marsh grasses that dapple in the wind like the Gulf itself—prairie tremblant, they call it—its tracks only an occasional *trainasse,* a trail cut for a pirogue, and the twisting network of bayous that run sluggishly to the four points of the compass and drain finally into the Gulf."

Shirley Ann Grau, The Hard Blue Sky, *1955*

Tangled in Deep by Simon B. Gunning, 1990. A native of Australia, Gunning fell in love with New Orleans on a visit and moved there in 1981. He soon began painting Louisiana's natural landscapes, in which he finds a kinship with the Australian bush. In both, he says, "there is a curious sense of the hostile and the beautiful." *Ogden Museum of Southern Art*

Forest and Prairie

Northern and north-central Louisiana form a distinct geographical region, formally known as the Gulf Slope but more colloquially called the Pine Belt. Here is rolling hill country, punctuated by bluffs and thickly wooded with hickory, magnolia, pine, and 15 species of oak. Through the 18th century, timber was a main source of revenue for the Louisiana colony.

South of the Pine Belt lie grasslands, or prairies, extending west to the Calcasieu River and Lake Charles. This is Louisiana's rice bowl, producing one-fourth of the nation's rice crop. And it is cattle country, in some ways more reminiscent of Texas and the Southwest than of the Deep South. Here, though, cattle ranches go by their French name, *vacheries,* and the cowboys are Cajuns—descendants of French settlers in Nova Scotia who made their way south to Louisiana in the mid-1700s.

A Southern Stream by George David Coulon, 1892. Coulon painted landscapes throughout the state, including this uplands vista of a clear, unspoiled brook. *Roger Houston Ogden Collection*

"THE BEAUTIFUL COUNTRYSIDE IS BLANKETED BY WOODS, containing all varieties of trees...."

Pierre le Moyne, Sieur d'Iberville, in his journal of a 1699 expedition to the lower Mississippi

Lone live oak in pasture near White Castle, Louisiana. Photograph by William Guion. *Courtesy the artist. Below: Trumpet Creeper* by Jean Andrews, c. 1985–90. This flowering vine grows wild in Louisiana's woods and fields, and it is also used ornamentally. *University of North Texas Press*

I saw in Louisiana a live-oak growing,

All alone stood it and the moss hung down from the branches,
Without any companion it grew there uttering joyous leaves of
   dark green
And its look, rude, unbending, lusty, made me think of
   myself…

       Walt Whitman, from "I Saw in Louisiana a Live-Oak Growing," 1860

Hurricane Betsy in 1965 wrought havoc throughout the state. Here, in New Orleans's famous French Quarter, debris lies on St. Peter Street in front of the Pontalba Apartments, the oldest apartments in America. *Corbis-Bettmann*

Several times a decade, hurricanes rise in the Atlantic and sweep through the Caribbean into the Gulf of Mexico, striking the Louisiana coast with devastating force. The first recorded hurricane, in 1722, destroyed most of the buildings in the fledgling city of New Orleans. Journalist Lafcadio Hearn re-created the hurricane of August 10, 1856, in his short novel *Chita: A Memory of Last Island.* But that storm was puny compared to the 1893 cyclone that destroyed a barrier island known as Cheniere Caminada and killed more than half its population. By the 20th century, hurricanes bore names—Betsy, Audrey, Camille, and Andrew all took their toll on Louisiana—and the new science of meteorology was starting to predict them. The first real hurricane warnings in history were sent to New Orleanians before a destructive 1915 storm.

Even more calamitous was the periodic flooding of the Mississippi and its tributaries. Originally the rivers overflowed their banks every year during the spring rains. Later a system of earthen levees prevented this natural cycle from destroying valuable farmlands. ❧

"IT WAS STIFLINGLY HOT.... THE RAIN WAS COMING DOWN IN sheets obscuring the view of far-off cabins and enveloping the distant wood in a gray mist. The playing of the lightning was incessant. A bolt struck a tall chinaberry tree at the edge of the field. It filled all visible space with a blinding glare and the crash seemed to invade the very boards they stood upon."

Kate Chopin, "The Storm," 1898

What has happened down here, is the winds have changed;
    clouds roll in from the north and it starts to rain.
Rained real hard and it rained for a real long time;
    six feet of water in the streets of Evangeline.

"Louisiana 1927," words and music by Randy Newman, 1974

Ship Natchez of New Orleans, Scudding Under a Reefed Foresail and a Close Reefed Mainsail by James F. Pringle, 1832. A violent storm on the Gulf of Mexico is the subject of this dramatic seascape by the British-born marine painter. *Ogden Museum of Southern Art*

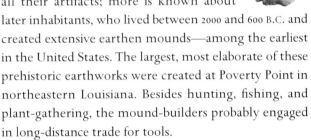

Right: Natchez fishtail arrow point c. A.D. 800–1000. *Below:* Mound A at the Poverty Point site. *Both, Louisiana State Exhibit Museum Opposite above: Louisiana Indians Walking Along a Bayou* by Alfred L. Boisseau, 1847. The hairstyles and baskets indicate that these are Choctaws, probably from near Lake Pontchartrain. *New Orleans Museum of Art. Opposite below:* Distinctively etched pot made by Tunica people in the mid-18th century. *Peabody Museum, Harvard University*

The First Louisianians

"Paleo-Indians" established communities in what is now Louisiana 12,000 years ago. Using stone-tipped spears, these early natives hunted camels, giant armadillos, mastodons, ground sloths, and long-horned bison in the cool forests and grasslands. Rising sea levels and humidity erased nearly all their artifacts; more is known about later inhabitants, who lived between 2000 and 600 B.C. and created extensive earthen mounds—among the earliest in the United States. The largest, most elaborate of these prehistoric earthworks were created at Poverty Point in northeastern Louisiana. Besides hunting, fishing, and plant-gathering, the mound-builders probably engaged in long-distance trade for tools.

By the time of French colonization in the early 17th century, about 13,000 to 15,000 Indians lived in Louisiana, their numbers already depleted by war and by diseases transmitted from the Europeans. Major tribal groups included the Caddo and Tunica in the north; Natchez, Atakapa, and Muskhogee in central Louisiana; and Chitimacha in the south. They lived in

villages, cultivating corn, beans, and squash, and hunting
deer, wild turkeys, and waterfowl. To navigate the bayous,
they made dugout canoes from cypress trunks; the
French called them pirogues and adopted the concept. ❦

"FIRST THERE WAS NOTHING BUT WATER, HIDING THE
earth everywhere. The Great Spirit made fish and
shellfish to live in the water. Then he told Crawfish to dive under the water and bring up mud to
make the earth. As soon as Crawfish had done
this, the Great Spirit made men. He called the earth
and the men 'Chitimacha.'"

From The Indians of Louisiana, *by Fred Kniffen, 1945*

Between France and Spain

A Spaniard, Hernando de Soto, was the first European to set foot on Louisiana land, in 1542. Nearly 150 years passed before other Europeans—Frenchmen this time—ventured into the region. Embarking from Canada, René-Robert Cavelier, Sieur de la Salle, reached the mouth of the Mississippi in 1682; upon arriving, he proclaimed possession of "Louis' land" (La Louisiane) in the name of Louis XIV. It was a vast territory, bordered by the Rockies and the Alleghenies and watered by the Mississippi and its tributaries. But for decades Louisiana's importance remained mostly strategic—a geopolitical buffer against England. Its only settlements were forts; its first city, New Orleans, was not founded until 1718. African slaves arrived a year later, deposited by the Company of the Indies, a land-speculation business run for France by a Scotsman, John Law.

Despite Law's promises that the colony would yield great riches, Louisiana was an economic drain on the French empire. Tobacco and indigo crops failed, Indians waged wars, slaves rebelled. In 1763, as part of the Treaty of Paris that ended the French and Indian War, France gave Louisiana to Spain. The Spaniards were no more successful at

Hernando de Soto, from an old print. Right: Père Antoine (Father Antonio de Sedella) by Edmund Brewster, 1822. This popular hero is depicted as an unassuming monk. Archdiocese of New Orleans, on loan to Louisiana State Museum Opposite above: Marianne Celeste Dragon, school of José de Salazar, c. 1795. Salazar, the colony's first important portraitist, gave his Creole subjects a certain grandeur. Louisiana State Museum Opposite below: Mural of La Salle claiming the Mississippi watershed for France. Color lithograph by Bocquin, c. 1860. Historic New Orleans Collection

making the colony profitable, but they did make it populous: 25 years after their takeover, Louisiana's population had nearly quintupled, to 39,410. More than half were African slaves; the Spanish also welcomed Acadians from French Canada, Isleños from the Canary Islands, and American loyalists during the Revolution. Despite Spain's successes, however, France had clearly won the cultural war: its language was spoken universally, and French customs such as Mardi Gras endured.

Creole Culture

The term "Creole" (the Spanish equivalent is *criollo*) eludes definition. It originally referred to the Louisiana-born descendants of the early French and Spanish colonists—in particular, their white descendants. Over the centuries, it was applied more loosely to some French-speaking mixed-race populations ("Creoles of color") as well as to any Catholic, non-Anglo-American families with deep roots in the colony. Creoles further stratified themselves into "Old Creoles" *sorti de la cuisse de Jupiter* ("a piece of Jupiter's thigh") and "countrified" Creoles, or Chacalatas.

"Show me any Creole…and right down at the foundation of it all, I will find you this same preposterous, apathetic, fantastic, suicidal pride. It is as lethargic and ferocious as an alligator."

George Washington Cable, The Grandissimes *(novel), 1880*

Portrait of a Free Woman of Color by Louis A. Collas, 1829. Before the Civil War, Louisiana had a sizable population of "free persons of color," who owned property, businesses, and even slaves. *Femmes de couleur* often acquired fortune and power through the Quadroon Balls, where they met rich planters who supported them in style. *New Orleans Museum of Art.* Right: *Playing Bourré* by George Rodrigue, 1979. *George Rodrigue Library*

"Café noir is their nectar, and Perique tobacco their ambrosia."

Samuel H. Lockett on the Cajuns

From Acadia

The ancestors of Louisiana's Cajuns left coastal France for Acadia in far northeastern Canada in 1604. And they likely would have remained in that harsh but beautiful land had not a British governor seen fit to expel them in the winter of 1755. His cruel and arbitrary edict, known among Cajuns as "Le Grand Dérangement," doomed half of the exiles to death at sea or in perilous overland journeys. But among the survivors were about 4,000 who found their way to Louisiana between 1760 and 1790. They and their descendants flourished in the isolated bayou country, pursuing a life of fishing, trapping, and hunting. Until

Evangeline by Alexandre Alaux, c. 1927. *Louisiana State Museum.* Although he never visited Louisiana, the New England poet Henry Wadsworth Longfellow left his mark on the state's mythmaking. His romantic idyll "Evangeline," about two star-crossed lovers who journey from Acadia (Nova Scotia) to St. Martin Parish in Louisiana, has been memorized by generations of schoolchildren and adapted into a Hollywood movie. Longfellow loosely based his tale on the true story of two Acadian exiles. Alaux's painting depicts the lovers meeting by the beautiful Evangeline Oak in St. Martinville.

well into the 20th century, many Cajuns spoke an archaic form of French and cultivated centuries-old folkways. Today their flavorful cuisine, infectious music, and ebullient love of life are an indelible part of the Louisiana character.

Thus ere another noon they emerged from the shades; and before them
Lay, in the golden sun, the lakes of the Atchafalaya.
Water-lilies in myriads rocked on the slight undulations
Made by the passing oars, and, resplendent in beauty, the lotus
Lifted her golden crown above the heads of the boatmen.

Henry Wadsworth Longfellow, "Evangeline," 1847

"Frankly, it costs us more than it is worth."

Mariano Luis de Urquijo, Spain's chief minister for foreign affairs, 1800

Louisiana Purchased

As a revenue source for the enfeebled Spanish empire, Louisiana was a fiasco. So it proved relatively easy for Napoléon, then emperor of France, to wrest back control of the colony through a secret 1800 treaty.

The French flag flew again over New Orleans for just 20 days: Napoléon's foreign minister, Talleyrand, had already arranged to sell the entire Louisiana Territory to the United States for the then staggering sum of $15 million.

The sale catapulted Louisiana into a foreign culture with a new language—English—and alien political traditions. Statehood was promised, but first came an eight-year probation, during which the territorial governor attempted to instill into the recalcitrant Creoles such Anglo-American values as trial by jury. Louisiana did not become truly Americanized

until the Battle of New Orleans—the last gasp of the War of 1812, in which Creoles, Cajuns, blacks, Choctaw Indians, and even a band of pirates led by the legendary Jean Lafitte joined forces to defeat the invading British. The victory brought national acclaim to Colonel Andrew Jackson and gave Louisianians their first starring role on the American stage.

"LET THE LOUISIANIANS KNOW THAT WE PART FROM THEM WITH regret. [Let them] recollect that they were Frenchmen, and that France, in ceding them, has secured for them advantages which they could not have obtained from a European nation, however paternal it might have been."

Napoléon Bonaparte

Battle of New Orleans by Dennis Malone Carter, 1856. Fought after the War of 1812 had officially ended, the Battle of New Orleans helped give Lousianians a sense of American identity. It also propelled Andrew Jackson onto the national stage. *Historic New Orleans Collection*

War and Reconstruction

The years between statehood and the Civil War were an era of prosperity and growth for Louisiana; cotton, sugar, and

Mississippi River trade made it one of the wealthiest states in the South. Such affluence was made possible only by a huge slave labor force—about half the state's population. With secession from the Union in 1861 and the start of hostilities in 1862, Louisiana began a downward slide that lasted nearly a century.

Louisiana's contributions to the War Between the States, however, were exceptional. Judah P. Benjamin, a West Indian Jew who had emigrated to Louisiana and served in the U.S. Senate, became known as "the brains of the Confederacy"; he held three posts in Jefferson Davis's cabinet. Two of the Confederacy's eight full generals were Louisiana natives. On the other side, some 24,000 Louisiana blacks—the most from any state—served in the Union army. So did several regiments of white Louisianians. The surrender at New Orleans on May 26, 1862—the last important Union victory—ushered in Reconstruction and its discontents: racial violence, political corruption, and near-anarchy. It was a disaster from which Louisiana would not fully recover until the mid-20th century.

Left: Sergeant Page M. Baker, Louisiana soldier, c. 1860s. Photographer unknown. *Museum of the Confederacy. Below:* Louisiana Tigers, c. 1863. This wooden box with carved bone overlay celebrates the Confederate victory at Bull Run under General P. G. T. Beauregard. It was made by Confederate prisoners of war. *Ogden Museum of Southern Art. Opposite above: Battle of Port Hudson on the Mississippi* by Edward E. Arnold, 1864. *Louisiana State University Museum of Art. Opposite below:* Flag of the 5th Louisiana Infantry. *Museum of the Confederacy*

"I HAVE NO STOMACH FOR A FIGHT IN WHICH I AM TO HAVE the choice between the man who denies me all my rights, openly and fairly [Lincoln], and a man who admits my rights but intends to filch them [Douglas]."

*U.S. Senator Judah P. Benjamin
on the 1860 Presidential campaign*

"THERE IS NO REORGANIZATION OF THE South but through a baptism of blood."

New Orleans Picayune *editorial, 1860*

> ## *"It takes a rich cotton planter to make a poor sugar planter."*
>
> *Old Louisiana saying*

Above: Wild Indigo; Dogg-wood Tree. **Engraving by M. van der Gucht.** *New York Public Library. Right: Comin' from the Market near Baton Rouge* **by William Aiken Walker, c. 1870s.** *The David Warner Foundation, Tuscaloosa, Alabama Opposite: Inside the New Orleans Cotton Office* **by Edgar Degas, 1873. The famous French painter came to New Orleans to visit his Creole relatives.** *Musée des Beaux-Arts/ Art Resource*

Cotton and Cane

Louisiana's economic fortunes are a saga of boom and bust—ironic, given the state's astonishing natural fertility. Despite it, French and Spanish colonizers failed at early attempts to profit from tobacco, olives, pineapples, and grapes. Only indigo (a plant yielding a blue dye) and rice came near succeeding, probably because similar species were familiar to the West African slaves who worked the crops. With more modest ambitions and without slave labor, German and Acadian immigrants created productive small farms; German farmers put food on New Orleans tables throughout the colonial period. But the leading model of agriculture was the

plantation, adopted from the French West Indies and adapted to two major crops: cotton and sugarcane.

Sugar was by far the more lucrative. The average antebellum sugar plantation was valued at $200,000, twice the worth of a cotton operation. Sugar became profitable in the late 1700s, when knowledgeable producers arrived from Haiti, fleeing slave insurrections there. At the height of the antebellum era, Louisiana supplied 95 percent of the nation's sugar. The Civil War and the Depression temporarily crippled the state's sugar industry; today, it has rebounded to rank third behind Hawaii and Florida.

Sweet Success

Norbert Rillieux, a free person of color born in 1806 in New Orleans and educated in France, revolutionized the production of sugar. His multiple-effect evaporator, patented in 1843, yielded far more high-quality sugar, using much less fuel, than had ever been possible. His invention became the basis of modern sugar milling.

"RICE PLANTING IS USUALLY CARRIED ON AMONG A number of friends, neighbors, or relatives in partnership. The heat, perspiration, and fatigue incident to rice cultivation are not considered very much in a crowd of friends who are their own bosses and cut their own rice in their own way. But to an outsider, $1.25 per day is demanded."

St. Charles Herald, *1883*

"MR. R. ASSURED ME THAT DURING THE LAST GRINDING-season nearly every man, woman, and child on his plantation, including his overseer and himself, were at work fully eighteen hours a day. From the moment grinding first commences, until the end of the season, it is never discontinued."

Frederick Law Olmsted's observations of a Louisiana sugar plantation, in A Journey in the Seaboard Slave States, *1856*

Rice Festival, Crowley by Theodore Fonville Winans, c. 1940. *Louisiana State Museum Right:* Workers bringing in sugarcane for grinding, *Harper's Weekly* illustration, 1883. *Hill Memorial Library, LSU Opposite above: A Plantation Burial* by John Antrobus, 1860. *Historic New Orleans Collection Opposite below: Mark Gale at Glendale Plantation.* Photograph by Chandra McCormick. *Courtesy the artist*

"THE DARK SUGAR HOUSE; THE BATTERY OF HUGE CALDRONS, with their yellow juice boiling like a sea, half-hidden in clouds of steam; the half-clad, shining negroes swinging the gigantic utensils with which the seething flood is dipped from kettle to kettle; here, grouped at the end of the battery, the Creole planters with anxious faces drawing around their central figure as closely as they can;...until in the moment of final trial, there is a common look of suspense and instantly after it, the hands are dropped, heads are raised, the brow is wiped, and there is a long breath of relief—'it granulates.'"

George Washington Cable on Etienne Bore's successful crystallization of sugar in 1795, in The Creoles of Louisiana, *1884*

During the late 19th and early 20th centuries there were dozens of local coffee brands that capitalized on New Orleans's position as the premier coffee port in the United States. *Private collection. Opposite: Port and City of New Orleans by Marie Adrien Persac, 1858. Historic New Orleans Collection*

The crescent bend in the Mississippi at New Orleans forms a natural harbor, and there the French built a port in 1718. It was the colony's lifeline, a conduit for Louisiana's exports to Europe—lumber, furs, some agricultural products—and eventually for imports from the northern and midwestern states. After the Louisiana Purchase, river trade soared. Flatboats, keelboats, and barges crowded the banks at New Orleans, bringing salt, coffee, and manufactured goods from the Caribbean, South America, and the North. The real breakthrough came in January 1812, when the first steamboat—the namesake *New Orleans*—arrived in the Crescent City. Here at last was a vessel that could navigate upriver as well as downstream. By the 1850s, more than 3,000 steamboats docked at New Orleans each year. The port quickly became the world's largest export center; in some antebellum years, the value of river and oceangoing shipments was close to $500 million—several times more than the federal budget. The Civil War ended this boomtime, but another began in 1914, after the opening of the Panama Canal. Suddenly the Port of New Orleans became a major terminus for ocean shipping—a position it still holds today. ❧

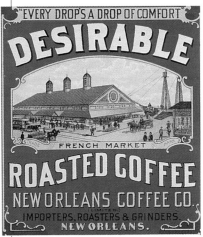

"EVERY DROP'S A DROP OF COMFORT"

DESIRABLE

FRENCH MARKET

ROASTED COFFEE

NEW ORLEANS COFFEE CO.
(LIMITED)

IMPORTERS, ROASTERS & GRINDERS.
NEW ORLEANS.

"The mighty mart of merchandise brought from more than a thousand rivers."

An 1801 description of the Port of New Orleans by visiting geographer William Darby

"LIKE ALL FOREIGNERS WHO VISIT THE GREAT LOUISIANA CITY, I WAS seized with admiration on seeing the activity which reigned on the docks....It is a world of commission men, speculators, and dealers who argue feverishly in the midst of this piled-up merchandise. Horses, wagons, negroes, and whites, bustled about in an area six hundred feet wide, where half the business of the United States takes place."

Henri Herz, French musician, on the New Orleans docks in 1846

Catfish and Crawfish

Aquatic life abounds in Louisiana. Pompano, trout, redfish, flounder, and crabs swim in the deep waters off the coast; the rivers and streams produce catfish, garfish, and the ubiquitous crawfish—also known as crayfish, crawdad, and mudbug. (The crawfish is in fact a crustacean whose American name comes from the French *écrevisse*.) The Bayou State produces more than 10 million pounds of oyster meat each year; Yugoslavian fishermen are credited with introducing oyster farming in the early 1800s. Louisiana is also the leading producer of fresh shrimp; the trawl, introduced in 1917, allowed large hauls of shrimp to be brought in from the Gulf of Mexico. A shrimp-drying process introduced by a Cantonese immigrant, Lee Yim, helped build an industry in Terrebonne Parish.

Above: Blue Crab and Terrapins by Achille Perelli, c. 1880. The Italian-born artist came to New Orleans in 1850. He remains best known for his natural-history studies, rivaling Audubon's in their precise detail. *New Orleans Museum of Art Right:* Wild oystering, near Leeville. *Photo Brian Gauvin*

"THE MISSISSIPPI FURNISHES IN GREAT PLENTY SEVERAL sorts of fish, particularly perch, pike, sturgeon, eel, and calts of a monstrous size. Craw-fish abound in this country; they are in every part of the earth."

Thomas Hutchins, a British military observer, 1784

Blessing of the Shrimp Fleet by France M. Folse, 1949. Folse painted flat, primitive scenes of events on Bayou Lafourche. In this painting, the priest and his acolytes are in the boat on the right; the dressed-up crowd watches from the shore. *Ogden Museum of Southern Art*

Black Gold

Beneath Louisiana's fertile lands and waters lay even greater wealth. The Natives knew about the thick black substance that seeped to the surface; the Spanish and French explorers used it to seal their boats. But not until 1866 did anyone try to drill an oil well—and that turned up dry. In 1901 the Spindletop gusher, near Jennings, changed everything. Further explorations uncovered rich deposits of oil and natural gas throughout the state; in the late 1930s oil fields were also found beneath the Gulf of Mexico. Oil wealth enabled the state to escape from chronic poverty; both Standard and Shell Oil are headquartered here. But bust followed boom: in 1985 oil prices plummeted and production fell sharply.

Oil rig in the Gulf of Mexico, 117 miles south of Intercoastal City. *Photo Brian Gauvin* *Opposite above: Avery Island Salt Mines* by Paul Ninas, 1934. A Missouri native, Ninas moved to New Orleans in 1932 and later established an art colony near Avery Island. *Ogden Museum of Southern Art. Opposite below:* One of Louisiana's many hot-sauce brands. *Sharon Dinkins Collection*

Salt of the Earth

Without salt, there would be no oil in Louisiana: as salt plugs surfaced from far below the earth, oil migrated upward with it. Louisiana salt has long been prized for its purity, abundance, and accessibility. Three of the world's largest salt mines are located in the Five Islands district near New Iberia; one of the most important is on Avery Island. Local salt together with the local peppers inspired Avery Island's most famous product: Tabasco sauce, the fiery red potion found in kitchens around the world. Avery Island and the Tabasco company have been owned since 1868 by the McIlhenny family, which maintains the 250-acre island as a wildlife and waterfowl sanctuary.

"THE PERFECT BLACKNESS OF THE CAVITIES, the extreme brilliancy of the edges which catch the light, and the wonderful intricacy of the innumerable curves made by the intersection of so many surfaces give to all of this subterranean scene a dazzling, weird, trembling brilliancy that looks more like enchantment than reality."

Samuel H. Lockett on the Avery salt mine, 1876

Second Ursulines Convent and Priest's House by William Woodward, 1912. The original convent, established in 1727, was the first convent and girls' school in the United States. *New Orleans Museum of Art.* Opposite above: *Her First Communion* by Josephine Marien Crawford, 1935. *New Orleans Museum of Art* Opposite below: *Panorama of Baptism on Cane River* by Clementine Hunter, c. 1945. Often called "the black Grandma Moses," the self-taught Hunter was born in 1886 or 1887, and painted full-time from the 1940s up to her death at the age of 101. This oil painting was made on a window shade. *Ogden Museum of Southern Art*

Catholic in Every Sense

Unlike the British colonies in America, colonial Louisiana not only had a state religion, it also had an official policy of non-tolerance. The *Code Noir,* enacted by the French court in 1724, prohibited the practice of any religion other than Roman Catholicism. Yet compared with the Puritan colonies, Louisiana wore its religion lightly. No church existed in New Orleans until 1727, when the St. Louis Cathedral was completed. And observance tended toward the perfunctory; like Europeans, Louisianians attended Mass on Sunday morning and socialized the rest of the day. Protestants gained a toehold in 1805, and today form a majority in most northern parishes.

Jews began arriving in the 1820s, mostly from France and Germany. Since the mid-1970s, Louisiana's spiritual gumbo has been flavored by Vietnamese immigrants, both Buddhists and Catholics. Roman Catholicism's influence remains largely cultural, seen in the blessing of the fishing fleets in bayou towns, in the Italian community's observance of St. Joseph's Day, and in Mardi Gras festivities.

"A SABBATH IN NEW ORLEANS! HERE THE NOISIEST day of the week—so full of strange contrasts... of the grave and gay, saints and sinners.... It is not the Sabbath of New England."

Henry Didimus, New Orleans As I Found It, *1845*

Permanent Address by Marion Souchon, c. 1940–50. *New Orleans Museum of Art. Opposite above:* An above-ground tomb in St. Louis Cemetery No. 2 in New Orleans. The cast-iron winged hourglasses are symbols of the passage of time. Both St. Louis Cemeteries were founded during yellow fever epidemics and located where victims could be safely isolated. *Photo Mason Florence. Opposite below:* Brass band playing in a jazz funeral. *Photo Syndey Byrd*

Cities of the Dead

"A NEW ORLEANS CEMETERY IS A CITY IN MINIATURE, STREETS, curbs, iron fences, its tombs above ground....Little two-story dollhouses complete with doorstep and lintel."

Walker Percy, The City of the Dead, 1984

If life in sub-sea-level New Orleans was difficult, death was equally challenging. During the city's early years, interred coffins had a disturbing habit of floating up to the surface during floods and severe rainstorms. The Creoles' solution to this grave dilemma was to build freestanding tombs above the ground. These crypts, called *fours* because of their ovenlike appearance, took the appearance of miniature houses without windows, and the cemeteries became known as "Cities of the Dead." Forty-two of these cities, in various stages of repair and disrepair, dot the New Orleans cityscape. The oldest, built in 1788, is St. Louis Cemetery No. 1, just beyond the French Quarter. All of the cemeteries come to life, as it were, on All Saints' Day, November 1, when family members clean and decorate the tombs of their relatives—and often stay for a picnic. Other days of the year, the cemeteries are considered unsafe for solo touring and are best viewed in one of the city's many guided tours.

"IN NEW ORLEANS, THE JAZZ FUNERALS OF important members of the black community are shining models of respect and remembrance. The deceased are seen off by musical bands, followed by dancing friends, acquaintances, and strangers....Surely, people who show their affection in this way have a friend in the next world."

Andrei Codrescu in Elysium: A Gathering of Souls, 1997

Voodoo, or *voudon*, is a mixture of West African religious beliefs, notably ancestor worship. Introduced to Louisiana by African slaves, it received a large boost after the arrival, between 1809 and 1810, of some 9,000 refugees—including slaves and free blacks—from French Saint-Domingue, where voodoo was extremely popular. The practice flourished in New Orleans, regarded as the birthplace of North American voodoo. Throughout the 19th century, both whites and blacks consulted voodoo priests and priestesses to cure an illness, further an *amour*, or put a *gris-gris*—magic charm—on an enemy. By 1873, according to the *New Orleans Picayune*, there were 300 high priests and priestesses in the city. The most notorious was Marie Laveau, a free mulatto whose dramatic rituals included a snake-handling saturnalia every June 23, St. John's Eve. One of her daughters, also named Marie, inherited the title of "Voodoo Queen" and practiced the religion, some say, well into the 20th century. ⚜

Black Witchcraft

To hurt an enemy, put his name in a dead bird's mouth and let the bird dry up. This will bring him bad luck.

To drive a woman crazy, sprinkle nutmeg in her left shoe every night at midnight.

To keep your neighbor in a constant state of disappointment, take a piece of earth from a graveyard and throw it in his yard.

From Gumbo Ya-Ya, 1945

"GENERALLY [SHE WORE] A DRESS OF JENNY-BLUE calico—skirt made very full—a kerchief 'round her neck and a *tignon* or headdress, large hoop earrings of gold, some beads, and a brooch. She went on the streets as unconcerned as any washerwoman, smiling and often speaking to those she met. Whenever she was seen, people would stand aside and whisper, 'Here comes Marie Laveau,' and wait until she passed. But her power—it seemed supernatural! She worked with charms and herbs and incense and snakes and skeletons, and invoked spirits."

Former slave N. H. Hobley,
a contemporary of Marie Laveau

Above: Portrait of Marie Laveau by Charles Gandolfo, c. 1977. *New Orleans Historic Voodoo Museum. Photo Don Smetzer. Left:* Cleansing ceremony, New Orleans Voodoo Spiritual Temple, 1996. Participants circle a drawing representing serpent spirits of life, death, and rejuvenation. Mambo (Priestess) Miriam Williams leads the ceremony. *Photo David Blumenfeld. Opposite above:* Voodoo Museum exhibits. *Photo Robert Holmes/Corbis*

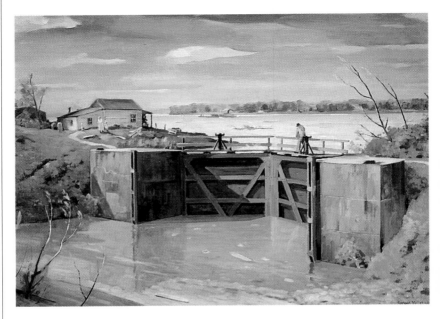

Violet Locks by Clarence Millet, 1950. Born in Hahnville, Millet apprenticed to a New Orleans engraver in 1914. He lived for the rest of his life in the Vieux Carré, and worked in the WPA's easel project in the 1930s. *Ogden Museum of Southern Art*

Taming the River

To live in Louisiana is to live with—or against—the whims of the Mississippi. Flooding is part of the river's natural cycle but is inconvenient (or worse) to permanent settlements. By 1731 the French colonial government had built a continuous levee along both banks of the Mississippi above New Orleans, but a 1735 flood destroyed most of it. The struggle continued after statehood and during the Civil War; not until the 1880s, when the Army Corps of Engineers intervened, were the levees built scientifically. Still, it took the Great Flood of 1927 to

"Man cannot tame that lawless stream....

One might as well bully the comets in their courses...as try to bully the Mississippi into right and reasonable conduct."

Mark Twain, 1883

prove that levees alone were not enough. A spillway down-river from Bonnet Carré, a historically dangerous bend in the stream, was completed in 1932 and so far has held back the Mississippi even in serious floods.

The river has also shaped the development of public roads. In 1732 French colonists built the Chemin Royal (Royal Road) behind the levees. Rechristened the River Road, the winding thoroughfare—once dirt, then gravel—was the only over-land route between New Orleans and Baton Rouge until 1935, when U.S. 61 was completed, a legacy of Governor Huey Long's ambitious highway program. Lined with majestic or ruined plantation homes, the River Road remains one of the most scenic routes in the country.

"THE MAINTENANCE OF THE LEVEES interests all the inhabitants where crevasses ruin in an instant the fruits of a year of labor.... Messrs. the syndics, will make forthwith a rigid examination of the levees of their district and will assign to each inhabitant the work that he will have to do there as soon as the crops will be finished...."

Gov. Carondelet's Levee Ordinance, 1792

Under the direction of a Union army officer, "contrabands" (former slaves) build a levee just downriver from Baton Rouge. Engraving from *Frank Leslie's Illustrated Newspaper,* 1863. *Courtesy Fred Benton Collection*

French Quarter Scene by Alson Skinner Clark, 1911. These 1830s buildings are on Decatur Street near Toulouse. The French Quarter survives thanks to farsighted citizens, who voted in the 1920s to preserve its architectural integrity. Restoration began in the 1970s under the eye of the Vieux Carré Commission. *Ogden Museum of Southern Art. Below:* The streetcar named Desire, 1945. *Historic New Orleans Collection*

A Streetcar Named...

"THEY TOLD ME TO TAKE A STREET-CAR NAMED DESIRE, AND THEN TRANSFER to one called Cemeteries and ride six blocks and get off at—Elysian Fields!"

Blanche DuBois in Tennessee Williams's A Streetcar Named Desire, *1947*

Though several of the trains Blanche DuBois rode are defunct, New Orleans remains justly proud of its streetcars, which ran long before roads were paved. The St. Charles Avenue line, which began operation in 1835, is the oldest operating urban railway system in the country. The cars in use today were built in the 1920s; they provide a fascinating and scenic tour of the city's Garden District.

JACKSON SQUARE, NEW ORLEANS, LA.—24
ST. LOUIS CATHEDRAL

PONTALBA BLDG. THE CABILDO STATE HISTORICAL MUSEUM

Old postcard of Jackson Square; the "State Industrial Museum" is now part of the Louisiana State Museum. *Private collection. Below:* Statue of Andrew Jackson by Clark Mills in New Orleans's Jackson Square. This is the world's first equestrian statue in which the horse has more than one foot off the base. *Photo Robert Holmes/ Corbis*

Preservation and Recreation

Louisiana's first public buildings were religious and governmental: the Ursulines Convent, built in 1752; the Cabildo, the seat of Spanish rule, built between 1795 and 1803. Few other structures survive from those early years, largely because fires and hurricanes destroyed much of New Orleans. Most of the French Quarter, also known as the Vieux Carré ("old quarter"), dates from the early to middle 19th century. In the late 20th century Louisiana looked to the future as well as to the past. Awakening to the potential of tourism and conventions, New Orleans embarked on a building spree that included the world's largest indoor arena, the Superdome; a convention center and luxury hotels; and the lovely riverfront "Moonwalk," named for former mayor Moon Landrieu.

> *"Oh, hell, say I'm sui generis and let it go at that."*
>
> Huey P. Long

Every Man a King

The most colorful character in Louisiana's colorful political history was Huey P. Long—the "Kingfish"—a charismatic dictator who rose to power through populist rhetoric, progressive reform, and political strong-arming. In Catholic, New

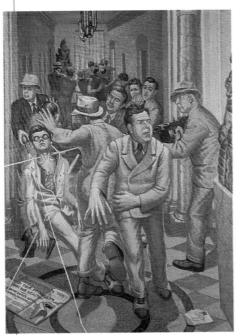

Orleans-dominated, oil-booming Louisiana, Long was an unlikely champion: he was a Protestant from the rural north, and he bit the hand that fed the state—Standard Oil. A master of the folksy idiom, he turned the state's underclass of poor black and white sharecroppers and laborers into a devoted constituency. Elected governor in 1928, Long launched ambitious programs and survived an array of accusations to catapult into the U.S. Senate. Even from Washington, Long continued to rule through influence and outright machination. He spoke of running for president. But a political enemy put an end to his ambitions: on September 8, 1935, Huey Long was shot and killed in Baton Rouge.

"A DUMPY FIGURE, PLAIN AND PUDGY AS A POTATO, Huey had an Emmett Kelly face under a kinky scribbling of damp rusty hair, with a nose like a radish bulb and an oddly straight mouth like the hinged slot of a ventriloquist's dummy. His garb, even after he reached the Senate, ran toward white suits with pink neckties and orange hand-kerchiefs, fawn and lavender silk shirts, and brown shoes trimmed in white—he resembled a walking dish of fruit ambrosia. At the same time, he was the sort of chap who would get into fracases in the men's rooms of nightclubs."

Marshall Frady, Southerners: A Journalist's Odyssey, *1980*

> Every man a king,
> Every man a king,
> For you can be a millionaire....
> There's enough for all people to share.
>
> *"Every Man a King," lyrics by Huey Long*

Above: Huey and President Smith, Baton Rouge, Louisiana by Theodore Fonville Winans, 1935. Senator Long with the president of Louisiana State University. Ogden Museum of Southern Art Left: Still photo from the movie Blaze, starring Paul Newman as Governor Earl K. Long and Lolita Davidovich as Blaze Starr. Earl, Huey's brother, served two terms as governor despite a very public affair with a striptease artist. And Huey's nephew Russell—Earl's son—served in the U.S. Senate. Photofest. Opposite: The Shooting of Huey Long by John McCrady, 1939. Long staggers in the foreground while his assassin, Dr. Carl A. Weiss, Jr., is pumped full of bullets. Courtesy Mr. and Mrs. Keith C. Marshall

The Creole Legacy

The first European-style dwellings in Louisiana were simple wood-framed structures filled in with *bousillage*, a mixture of mud and indigenous Spanish moss. Elevating houses on piers, a mode adapted from the Caribbean colonies, provided some relief from floods and mosquitoes. Stone was nonexistent in southern Louisiana, so later

The allée of oaks at Oak Alley Plantation. *Photo Owen Franklin. Right:* Hexagonal *garçonnière* at Houmas House Plantation, one of two that flank the main house. It was considered improper for Creole bachelors to stay in the same house as unmarried women. *Photo William Guion*

colonists substituted soft-baked brick as filling between wall posts; the *briqueté entre poteaux* style can still be seen in New Orleans's Vieux Carré.

As the colony prospered, distinctive embellishments emerged: a three-sided gallery (porch), an internal chimney, a spreading umbrella roof.

The resulting Creole hybrid is considered by architectural historians to be the only American colonial style that actually emerged in this country. Grander examples, including River Road plantations such as Laura and Magnolia Mound, put the main living quarters on the second story, safe from flooding; brick or wood-frame slave quarters stretched out behind the "big house." Some versions incorporated *garçonnières* (bachelor quarters) and *pigeonniers* (dovecotes). More modest dwellings—for example, the many urban "shotgun" cottages—provided maximum living space with minimal use of materials. ✤

Above: Maison Pontchartrain, Nouvelle Orléans by Nicolino Calyo, 1848. The Greek Revival style of the nearer house was unusual for New Orleans; the house in the background was built in the older Federal style. *Ogden Museum of Southern Art. Left:* The grand ballroom at Nottoway Plantation. Completed in 1859, this 64-room Italianate mansion featured such innovations as gas lamps, coal fireplaces, and indoor plumbing. It was restored in 1980 and is open to the public. *Photo Bernard Boutrit*

Wrought-iron balconies in the French Quarter. *Photo David Muench/ Corbis. Below:* Silver chalice by Adolphe Himmel, 1848. German silversmiths made New Orleans an important center of the craft until the Civil War. An inscription on the chalice refers to a militia of German-born citizens. *Louisiana State Museum*

Artistry in Iron

Graceful, often fanciful wrought-iron railings, fences, and gates are the decorative signature of New Orleans's French Quarter. Unlike cast iron, which replaced it around the middle of the 19th century, wrought iron is handcrafted and highly individual; cast iron, which is extremely brittle because of its high carbon content, must be formed ("cast") in molds. Wrought iron is a mostly anonymous art, but several accounts suggest that skilled black slaves were the principal authors, having brought the craft with them from West Africa, where ironworking had been highly developed for centuries before the slave trade. Other wrought-iron artisans included free men of color and Irish immigrants.

"THE STAIRCASE, WHICH RISES IN a gentle curve to the second story, is particularly fine, with its balustrade of hand-hammered ironwork. Like the bolts, bars, and hinges, this railing was beaten into shape by negro blacksmiths in the city's forges. These 'brute negroes,' as they were called, were masters of their craft, and throughout the old section of the city, one finds that the oldest ironwork is the most beautifully wrought."

Lyle Saxon, describing the old Ursulines convent, in Fabulous New Orleans, *1928*

Interior of the residence of conceptual artist Elizabeth Shannon, located in a former temperance hall in the Faubourg Marigny, New Orleans. Designed by the artist, the room contains a Victorian daybed draped with mosquito netting and a large painting by Dub Brock of Mississippi from his cane fields series. *Photo Richard Sexton Left:* Louisiana-crafted table from the Poydras Home for Older Women. *Louisiana State Museum*

The gardens and main house at Longue Vue, New Orleans. Created in the 1930s by landscape design doyenne Ellen Biddle Shipman for cotton planter Edward Stern, the gardens included many water features along with ornamental and kitchen gardens. *Photo Richard Sexton*

"Everything Grows Luxuriantly"

The semitropical lushness of Louisiana's climate made the state an Eden for gardeners. From colonial days, even modest city town houses had small courtyard gardens; where land was plentiful, gardens took wildly imaginative forms. Formal gardens were preferred, in the French style, but a freer style could be glimpsed in Valcour Aimé's legendary "Le Petit Versailles," near Vacherie. In the mid-19th century, Louisiana was a botanical crossroads—plants from Asia, Europe, and New England found their way to the levees and into gardens. During the 1830s Martha Barrow Turnbull, the wife of a leading cotton planter, created a 17th-century French garden out of the wilderness that surrounded Rosedown Plantation; the camellias and azaleas she planted still thrive today. The Civil War temporarily halted such large-scale gardening, but the Victorian and Edwardian eras saw a revival. Within the next half-century, gardens and garden restoration again would become serious pursuits.

"ALL OF THE HOUSES HERE, EXCEPT SOME IN THE old town and centre streets, have gardens— not very extensive... but the soil and climate are such that everything grows luxuriantly. Magnolias, jessamines [jasmines], roses, oranges, lemons, loquats, and a hundred other things beautiful and good; and then the mocking birds and butterflies, and the pretty little chameleons!"

Amelia M. Murray, Letters from the United States, Cuba, and Canada, *1856*

Above: Hodges Gardens is the nation's largest privately owned horticultural parkland. Its centerpiece is an abandoned stone quarry, which owners A. J. and Nona Trigg Hodges transformed into formal gardens. *Photo Neil Johnson. Left:* A landscaped courtyard in New Orleans's French Quarter. This building, known as the Old Spanish Stables, was renovated in the 1950s by developer Clay Shaw, who gained notoriety for his association with JFK conspiracy theories. *Photo Richard Sexton*

A Love Affair with Food

It's possible, and pleasurable, to feast from morning to night on foods created in Louisiana. The cultures that thrived here—French, Acadian, Spanish, Italian, and African—produced a unique cuisine and an unalloyed enthusiasm for the pleasures of the table. Begin the day with calas, the hot rice fritters once sold by singing street vendors in New Orleans's French Quarter, and still served at the Old Coffee Pot restaurant. Or sample a puffy beignet—the hot doughnuts made famous a century ago at Café du Monde—and wash it down with chicory coffee. (Roasted chicory grain originally was added when coffee was scarce; today the blend is preferred by many Louisianians.) Around midday, indulge in a muffuletta, the distinctive sandwich invented by Italian immigrants, or a fried oyster po' boy on French bread. Happy hour calls for a bourbon-and-bitters Sazerac (reputed to be the first cocktail) or a Ramos Gin Fizz, both invented in New Orleans saloons. For a casual dinner, enjoy a bowl of okra-thickened gumbo or seafood jambalaya; a more elegant evening might include Oysters Rockefeller, created at Antoine's in New Orleans in 1899. A dish of flaming Bananas Foster, created at Brennan's Restaurant, or a pecan praline (say *PRAH-leen*) will satisfy the most demanding sweet tooth.

"As delicious as the less criminal forms of sin."

Mark Twain on pompano cooked in Louisiana

"BREAKFAST IS SERVED: THERE IS ON THE table a profusion of dishes—grilled fowl, prawns, eggs and ham, fish from New Orleans, potted salmon from England, preserved meats from France, claret, iced water, coffee, and tea, varieties of hominy, mush and African vegetable preparations."

William Howard Russell describing a typical River Road plantation meal, 1860

Oysters Rockefeller

½ lb. spinach, washed well
6 or 8 scallions
½ head lettuce
1½ stalks celery
½ bunch parsley
1 clove garlic
1 cup butter
½ cup fine bread crumbs
1 tbsp. Worcestershire sauce
1 tsp. anchovy paste
½ tsp. salt
Few dashes Tabasco sauce
2 tbsp. absinthe or Pernod
36 oysters

Chop finely or grind together vegetables. Heat butter and mix in all but the oysters. Refrigerate. Spoon mixture onto 36 oysters on the half shell, set the oyster halves on a bed of rock salt, and bake in a hot oven (450° F) until piping hot. Serve immediately.

Two of Louisiana's most influential artists were Yankee brothers who arrived in New Orleans in the 1880s. Massachusetts native William Woodward came to the 1884 World's Industrial and Cotton Centennial Exposition as a drawing instructor; his brother Ellsworth followed soon after. When the H. Sophie Newcomb College for young women opened in 1886, both brothers joined the staff, William in the architecture department and Ellsworth as director of the art program. Under the Woodwards' guidance, Newcomb's pottery program became internationally famed; the pottery itself—made from local clay and decorated by the female students with images of Louisiana flora and fauna— is highly collectible today. Noted painters in

Above: Iris Field Near Newcomb Greenhouse by Ellsworth Woodward, 1911. *Right: Newcomb Vase with Magnolias, Newcomb Vase with Palm and Moon* by Sadie A. E. Irvine, 1930 and 1923. Irvine was one of the best-known and most prolific of the Newcomb College ceramicists; like the other Newcomb artists, she used local clay and decorated her pieces with images of Louisiana flora. *Both, Ogden Museum of Southern Art*

Woodward House, Lower-line and Benjamin Streets by William Woodward, 1899. *Historic New Orleans Collection.* Below: *Portrait of William Woodward* by Ellsworth Woodward, c. 1910. *New Orleans Museum of Art*

their own rights, the Woodwards were also instrumental in persuading sugar tycoon Isaac Delgado to donate funds to build the Delgado Museum of Art in New Orleans's City Park; Ellsworth Woodward became the museum's first director. Known today as the New Orleans Museum of Art, the Delgado helped transform New Orleans into a mecca for local, national, and international artists, who flocked to the city in the 1920s and 1930s. ❧

> *"Louisianians have four great passions:*
> *food, football, music, and politics."*
>
> James Carville

Bon Temps Rouler

Blessed by climate and unburdened by the Puritan work ethic, early Louisianians embraced the pleasure principle to a degree unimaginable in other American colonies. The French and Spanish colonizers took their cue from the Native Americans, who indulged in elaborate dances, spirited gambling, and stickball games. The Europeans enthusiastically adopted all of these, and added their own traditions such as billiards, duels, promenades, and horse racing. And drinking: by 1791, New Orleans boasted one tavernkeeper for every 71 residents; the ratio in Philadelphia was 1 to 429. The pursuit of pleasure became so fevered that at various times colonial governors—and, once, the French court—tried to ban gambling, but failed utterly.

For participant and spectator alike, Louisiana offers an embarrassment of sporting riches. The fishing is superb, in river, lake, or gulf; the hunting—especially of waterfowl—is outstanding. But the true state sport is unquestionably football. College and bowl games draw thousands of fans. And even before the New Orleans Saints arrived in 1967, Louisiana contributed more than its share of players to the professional game, from "Red" Cagle in the 1920s to Terry Bradshaw more recently. ✿

Below: New Orleans Ladies by Seymour Fogel, 1938. Fogel, a New Yorker, visited New Orleans between 1938 and 1941 and produced several drawings and gouaches of French Quarter prostitutes. Storyville, the infamous red-light district, at its heyday boasted 230 houses of prostitution. It was officially closed after World War I, but New Orleans was still known for its pleasures of the flesh. Ogden Museum of Southern Art Opposite: Poker Game on a Riverboat by William Aiken Walker, 1880. Collection Jay P. Altmayer, Mobile, Alabama

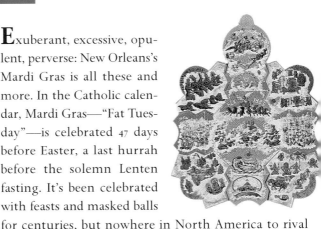

Right: Invitation to a 19th-century Mardi Gras ball. *Below:* Sketch of a Mardi Gras float for Comus Krewe, c. 1890s. By 1900 there were several all-black krewes taking part in Mardi Gras, and by 1917 the first all-female krewe had joined the ranks. Today there are dozens of krewes, from Barkus (a canine krewe) to Tucks to Zulu to the Phunny Phorty Phellows. *Both, Louisiana State Museum*

Exuberant, excessive, opulent, perverse: New Orleans's Mardi Gras is all these and more. In the Catholic calendar, Mardi Gras—"Fat Tuesday"—is celebrated 47 days before Easter, a last hurrah before the solemn Lenten fasting. It's been celebrated with feasts and masked balls for centuries, but nowhere in North America to rival New Orleans. Oddly, it took six Protestants from Mobile, Alabama, to launch Mardi Gras as it's known today. Calling themselves the Mistick Krewe of Comus, these newcomers formed a secret society in 1857 and mounted a masked ball for 3,000 at the Gaiety Theatre. They also created two lavish parade floats lit by *flambeaux* (burning torches). Comus ruled Mardi Gras unopposed until 1872, when the krewes of Momus (named for the god of mockery) and Rex were formed; Proteus came along a decade later. All four original krewes are still going

Ostentatious costumes are the rule during Mardi Gras. Masks, historical get-ups, and topical references are perennial favorites. *Photo Syndey Byrd*
Below: Rex, king of Mardi Gras, in 1901. *Collection Leonard V. Huber*

strong, throwing opulent balls that are among the hottest tickets in town. And Mardi Gras in New Orleans has become "the greatest free show on earth," with some 60 parades and myriad marching clubs filling the calendar between January 6—Twelfth Night—and Ash Wednesday. ❦

"THERE HE WAS—THE KING OF CARNIVAL, REX HIMSELF, the Monarch of Mirth, all in gold and positively exuding noblesse oblige....He was a well-padded gentleman, like most New Orleanians of a certain age, and he was in his element playing Old King Cole the merry old soul....The band in front of the float was playing 'When the Saints Go Marching In,' so Skip never heard the shot."

Julie Smith, New Orleans Mourning, *1990*

Les Mardi Gras è ou viens tu?
Tout a l'entour du fond d'hiver.

Mardi Gras, where do you come from?
Always around the bottom of winter.

Official song of Courir de Mardi Gras

Courir de Mardi Gras

Above: Gauntlet of gilded metal set with glass gemstones, worn by Rex in 1886. *Louisiana State Museum.*
Below: Courir de Mardi Gras. *Photo Danny Izzo*

Many cities and towns throughout the Bayou State adopt the New Orleans Mardi Gras style, with floats, parades, and marching bands. But in southwest Louisiana's Cajun country, the celebration takes a different form. Here costumed riders on horseback gallop wildly from farm to farm, staging mock raids for chickens and vegetables to make gumbo. The Courir de Mardi Gras—"running of Mardi Gras"—ends in the afternoon, and gumbo-making starts. Cajun dancing and feasting take up the rest of the evening. The tradition is thought to derive from the medieval *fête de la quémande,* a period of ceremonial begging in which French peasants played pranks on the gentry.

Mardi Gras Indians

Despite their name, the Mardi Gras Indians represent a black New Orleans tradition dating back to about 1880. During the 1790s some escaped slaves were taken in by local Chickasaws; the story of their alliance was passed down for generations, eventually finding expression in secret black "pleasure clubs" formed during Reconstruction. Today's Mardi Gras Indians—with names like Yellow Pocahontas, Wild Magnolias, and Wild Tchoupitoulas—are among Mardi Gras' most spectacular paraders. Their beaded and feathered costumes weigh up to 50 pounds.

"CLOUDS HUNG LOW THIS MARDI GRAS DAY OF 1940. King Zulu and his dukes sniffed heavenward. Let it rain. Little old water never hurt a mighty Zulu."

Lyle Saxon, Gumbo Ya-Ya, *1945*

Above: **Beadwork from a Mardi Gras Indians costume.** *Left:* **Mamut Montana of the Yellow Pocahontas club in full parade regalia.** *Photos Syndey Byrd*

Right: Ernest Gaines at River Lake Plantation, where he grew up in the black quarters. *Photo Marcia Gaudet*
Below: The house in New Orleans where William Faulkner lived in 1925 is now a bookstore. *Photo Robert Holmes/Corbis*

A Feast of Storytellers

Until well into the 19th century, Louisiana's literature was French literature, written first by members of exploring parties and later by Creoles educated in France. Vivid accounts of the new colony were contributed by a young Ursuline nun, Marie Madeleine Hachard, who arrived in 1727, in letters to her father in Rouen. From other pens came poems, novels, and histories that were avidly consumed by local and French audiences. But not until after the Civil War did Louisiana's writers gain recognition in this country. George Washington Cable's keenly observed tales of the Creole gentry, published in the 1870s and 80s, so incensed the local elite

that this New Orleans native decamped to New England. Visiting writers, from Walt Whitman, Mark Twain, and Lafcadio Hearn to William Faulkner and Tennessee Williams, found inspiration in Louisiana. Native sons and daughters also flourished—Ernest Gaines, with his powerful evocations of rural black life; John Kennedy Toole, whose *A Confederacy of Dunces* won a Pulitzer Prize; André Dubus, whose stories are gems of psychological realism. Among popular writers, James Lee Burke and Julie Smith have given to the whodunit a Louisiana accent, and Anne Rice has reinvented the gothic novel with her bestselling vampire cycle.

I must try to tell you what, in July, in Louisiana,
Night is....
...The night pants hot like a dog, it breathes
Off the blossoming bayou like the expensive whiff
Of floral tributes at a gangster's funeral in N.O.,
It breathes the smell love makes in darkness, and far off,
In the great swamp, an owl cries,...

Robert Penn Warren, from Selected Poems 1923–1975

Novelist and New Orleans native
Anne Rice with friend Arthur
Hardy at her home on St. Charles
Avenue. *Photo Syndey Byrd. Left:*
Portrait of playwright Tennessee
Williams by Leslie Staub, 1996.
Courtesy Le Mieux Galleries

Belles Lettres

Two important literary journals were
born in Louisiana. The *Double Dealer* lasted
only from 1921 to 1926, but it became
nationally acclaimed as "a magazine of
the moderns," publishing authors such
as Sherwood Anderson and Ernest Hem-
ingway. In 1935, the *Southern Review* took up
the banner. Its editors were Robert Penn
Warren and Cleanth Brooks; the first issue
included work by Aldous Huxley and
Ford Madox Ford. The *Southern Review*
continues to influence America's literati.

The French Opera House in New Orleans. *Historic New Orleans Collection. Right:* Cover of a libretto for Jules Massenet's *Herodias,* presented at the French Opera House in 1892. The cover advertises New Orleans's "leading milliner," on Canal Street. *Louisiana State Museum. Opposite:* A scene from *Hush, Hush, Sweet Charlotte,* filmed at Houmas House Plantation. *Shooting Star*

From Opera to Talkies

Decades before Bostonians and New Yorkers enjoyed regular theatrical performances, New Orleans was a vital center of drama and music. The city's first theater opened in 1792; the first opera—André Grétry's *Sylvain,* sung in French, of course—was performed in 1796. By the time the French Opera House opened in 1859, European singers and troupes were being imported for the opera season. Not all the talent came from afar. Ernest Guiraud, born in New Orleans in 1837, was sent to Paris for his musical education, returning for the premiere of his opera *Le Roi*

David at the tender age of 15. His achievements included completing Offenbach's unfinished *The Tales of Hoffman.* Louis Moreau Gottschalk was a piano virtuoso and a composer whose works—which integrate Creole, African-American, and other native melodies—are still performed. Another Louisiana prodigy, Shreveport-born pianist Van Cliburn, rocked the music world in 1958 when he won the International Tchaikovsky Competition in Moscow.

Louisiana pioneered in the popular arts as well: New Orleans's Vitascope was the first movie theater to open in the United States (in 1896), and the first talkie, *The Jazz Singer,* received its nation-wide premiere in New Orleans. Since then, many movies have been filmed in and about Louisiana.

Louisiana Filmography

Evangeline Silent film retelling of the Longfellow tale, with Dolores del Rio, 1927

Jezebel Civil War drama with Bette Davis, Leslie Howard, and a yellow fever epidemic in lead roles

King Creole Elvis Presley vehicle

Hush, Hush, Sweet Charlotte Bette again, with Joan Crawford on a crumbling Louisiana plantation

Pretty Baby Louis Malle's ode to Storyville, New Orleans's red light district, with Susan Sarandon and a young Brooke Shields

Blaze Title character was the stripper mistress of Gov. Earl K. Long, played by Paul Newman

The Big Easy Murder and police corruption in New Orleans, with Dennis Quaid and Ellen Barkin

JFK Oliver Stone's conspiracy epic

Belizaire the Cajun Armand Assante as a Cajun doctor in antebellum bayou country

Great Balls of Fire Biopic of native son and rock legend Jerry Lee Lewis

Eve's Bayou A girl's coming of age in the bayous

The Apostle Robert Duvall as an itinerant preacher and miracle worker

King Oliver's Creole Jazz Band, c. 1920–24. Influential bandleader and cornetist Joe "King" Oliver came from rural Louisiana to New Orleans in 1904. His sidemen here included Honore Dutrey on trombone, Baby Dodds on drums, Louis Armstrong (center front) on slide trumpet, and Armstrong's wife, Lil Hardin, on piano. *Hogan Jazz Archive, Tulane University Photo William Ransom*

Below: Sheet music for a Johnny Mercer tune in praise of Mardi Gras. *Private collection*

Louisiana's musical gift to the world emerged out of Storyville, the notorious New Orleans red-light district. Each of its many bordellos had at least one regular dance band. But jazz (or "jass," a slang term with sexual overtones) was already in the air by around 1900: in the up-tempos of marching brass bands, in the syncopations of ragtime piano, in the melodies of black minstrel performers, in the cadences of the Spanish Caribbean, and in the percussive rhythms that African slaves had preserved through their dances in Congo Square (now Louis Armstrong Park). Storyville piano player Jelly Roll Morton, a Creole of color whose real name was Ferdinand Le Menthe,

boasted that he created jazz singlehandedly; true or not, he was certainly the first important jazz composer and arranger. But he soon had intense competition from brilliant black (or Creole-of-color) jazz pioneers such as Kid Ory, Buddy Bolden, King Oliver, Sidney Bechet, and Louis Armstrong. White jazz bands also flourished—ironically, the term "jazz" was first applied to a white Chicago band in 1915. All of the early bands embodied a style now called "traditional" or "Dixieland" jazz, which emphasized clear melodic lines over complicated arrangements, and collective improvisation rather than solos. ❦

Left: Gospel pioneer Mahalia Jackson, a Louisiana native, at a recording session. *Corbis-Bettmann. Below:* The great Satchmo, Louis Armstrong, c. 1930s. *Underwood Photo Archives*

"WHEN I GOT MY FIRST JOB IN NEW ORLEANS PLAYING in a honky-tonk—Matranga's at Franklin and Perdido—I was 17, and it was same as Carnegie Hall to me. Yeah. Night I made my debut, I thought I was somebody. I took 15 cents home and I give it to my mother, and my sister woke up out of a sound sleep, say, 'Huh, blowing your brains out for 15 cents.' I wanted to kill her. Finally I got raised up to $1.25 a night—top money, man."

Louis Armstrong, in Life *magazine, 1966*

Zydeco

Another distinctively Louisiana sound is zydeco, the black counterpart to Cajun music. ("Zydeco" comes from the Cajun pronunciation of an old song title, "Les Haricots N'est Pas Salé"—"the beans aren't salty.") Blending traditional Cajun instruments like the accordion and the rub-board (a corrugated washboard worn on the chest) with electric guitar and African rhythm and blues elements, zydeco is infectiously uptempo and danceable. The late Clifton Chenier, a native of Opelousas, was largely responsible for bringing zydeco to a national audience in the 1970s and 1980s; John Delafose and the Eunice Playboys are among its current stars.

Zydeco master Clifton Chenier, whose distinctive accordion playing and vocals defined contemporary zydeco. *Photo Syndey Byrd. Right:* Charles Neville with his band, the Uptown All Stars, in 1997. As the Neville Brothers, Charles and his siblings, vocalists Aaron, Ivan, and Cyril, and keyboardist Art, created a uniquely Louisiana blend of R&B and soul. *Photo Richard Sexton*

"JAZZ I REGARD AS AN AMERICAN folk music; not the only one but a very powerful one which is probably in the blood and feeling of the American people more than any other style."

George Gershwin

Preservation Hall

Traditional New Orleans jazz was barely surviving in the late 1950s, when a new wave of cool, "listening" jazz dominated the clubs. But a handful of aficionados wouldn't let it die. In 1961 four white jazz enthusiasts began bringing in veteran musicians for jazz concerts in a rundown, dimly lit French Quarter art gallery. Word spread quickly, and soon the concerts were standing-room only. Thus was Preservation Hall born; today, still in the same building on St. Peter Street, it's a "living museum" of traditional jazz. Touring Preservation Hall bands have brought their inimitable sound around the world.

The first New Orleans Jazz & Heritage Festival was held in 1970 in Congo Square, a small park off the French Quarter where slaves had once gathered to play traditional instruments and dance. A few hundred people turned out that first year to hear Duke Ellington, Mahalia Jackson, and several traditional brass bands. Today, Jazz Fest draws a quarter of a million fans to a 35-acre site for 10 days in late April and early May. *Above:* Trumpeter Wynton Marsalis, of the New Orleans Marsalis clan, plays at Jazz Fest in 1989. *Left:* Bandleader Harold Dejan, c. 1980s. *Photos Syndey Byrd*

Right: Pond View by Elemore Morgan, Jr., 1992. Morgan, who hails from the rice fields and prairies outside Baton Rouge, paints directly from the land-scape on wide Masonite panels; his work captures the spacious horizons of his native country. *Arthur Roger Gallery.* Below: *Mourning Shadows* by Shirley Rabé Masinter, 1997. *Le Mieux Galleries*

Louisiana boasts a thriving contemporary art scene, rich in references to local themes yet universal enough to be appreciated by non-natives. For artists such as Mitchell Gaudet and Jeff Cook, assemblage is a means for expressing a sense of layered history—appropriate in a state where the past casts a long shadow. Cook's work includes subtle allusions to his African heritage. History also informs the sculpture of Clyde Connell, born in 1901 and active until her death at 97; she incorporated Indian shards and obsolete farm equipment into her tall, slender columns. Sometimes decadence rather than preser-

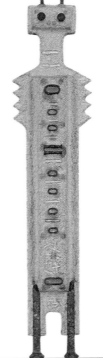

Treasures by Douglas Bourgeois, 1990. Into his small, shimmering, minutely detailed paintings, Bourgeois packs a world of ironic commentary on his native culture (that of southeast Louisiana) and the Roman Catholicism that is so much a part of its landscape. *Below: Figurative Wall Object* by Clyde Connell, 1993. *Both, Arthur Roger Gallery*

vation is the theme, as in George Dunbar's paintings, whose minimalism is slyly undermined by his opulent use of gold leaf. The late Ida Kohlmeyer took a more vibrant approach to painting and sculpture; her palettes reflect the brilliancy of Mardi Gras costumes.

Folk and "outsider" art also play an important role in Louisiana's art profile. One of the state's most important self-taught artists, Clementine Hunter, achieved international acclaim with her boldly rendered scenes of rural life. The descendant of slaves, Hunter picked cotton for years at Melrose Plantation; she took up painting in the 1940s almost on a whim, using paints left behind by a plantation visitor.

Somewhere between the conceptual artists and the outsiders is George Rodrigue, a Cajun from New Iberia who describes his work as "naive surrealism." Rodrigue achieved early success with charming paintings of Cajun life, and became a commercial phenomenon with his haunting "Blue Dog" series. ✤

Above: Seven-headed Dragon/Monster by David Butler. The self-taught Butler, born in 1898 in St. Mary Parish, still creates colorful sculpture in painted sheet iron. Ellin and Baron Gordon. Right: Novena for the Oaks by George Rodrigue, 1992. George Rodrigue Library

Composition 94-1 by Ida Kohlmeyer, 1994. *Arthur Roger Gallery.* Below: Chair by YA/YA artist Chris Peratore. The program was founded in 1988. *Courtesy YA/YA, Inc.*

YA/YA

In Creole patois, "ya-ya" means "oldest daughter." In New Orleans, YA/YA means Young Aspirations/Young Artists, an innovative art program that combines social service, artistic mentoring, and entrepreneurship. Artist Jana Napoli, a New Orleans native, taught painting techniques to students from an inner-city high school. Under her tutelage, the students began transforming flea-market chairs and chifferobes into vivid dreamscapes. The chairs became hugely successful with local collectors and have been exhibited in New York, Los Angeles, Europe, and Tokyo. YA/YA artists have been commissioned to design watches for Swatch; their splashiest project was a series of painted fabric covers for the chairs in the U.N. General Assembly. Their studio/gallery is located in New Orleans's Warehouse/Arts District at 628 Baronne.

Parish the Thought

Louisiana is the only state where counties are called "parishes," a legacy of the colonial Roman Catholic Church. The areas of some original parishes represent the territories served by early churches.

A Truly Super Dome

All superlatives really do apply to the Louisiana Superdome. The largest indoor arena in the world, it occupies a total land area of 52 acres, is as tall as a 27-story building, and can seat 76,000 fans for some sporting events and 87,500 for concerts. Its 166,000-square-foot concrete floor is covered with strips of AstroTurf—here renamed, appropriately, Mardi Grass.

Hey, Stella!

Aspiring Brandos test their lung power and histrionic flair at the "Stella and Stanley shouting contest," a featured event in the Tennessee Williams/New Orleans Literary Festival. Held each March to honor the author of *A Streetcar Named Desire,* it includes literary panels, staged productions, and walking tours.

This Town Is Hopping

Sixteen miles west of Lafayette, the town of Rayne proudly proclaims itself "The Frog Capital of the World." Every September there's a frog festival with frog races, frog beauty contests, and frog fireworks.

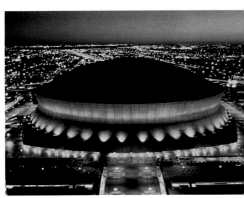

That Old Black Magic

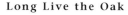

Charms, potions, human skulls—they're all on display, right out in the open, at the New Orleans Historic Voodoo Museum. Said to be the world's only private museum devoted to voodoo, it's crammed with the weird and the outré. Be advised: some of the exhibits are definitely not for the squeamish.

Long Live the Oak

There are tree-preservation societies all over, but Lafayette's Live Oak Society, founded in 1934, may be unique. For one thing, membership is limited to specimens at least 100 years old; for another, annual "dues" are 25 acorns. The live oak *(Quercus virginiana)* enjoys a special place in Louisiana folklore: to local Indians, its presence indicated high ground, safe from river flooding; later settlers found live oaks particularly well suited to lovers' trysts, duels, hangings, and treasure burials.

Bridge of Size

The Lake Pontchartrain Causeway, accessible from Interstate 10, is the world's longest overwater highway bridge. Completed in 1956, it crosses 23.8 miles of open water and takes passengers out of sight of land for eight miles. At mile marker 16 there's an opening span to accommodate ships.

Great People

A selective listing of native Louisianians, focusing on the arts.

Antoine "Fats" Domino (b. 1928), rock 'n' roll musician

Louis "Satchmo" Armstrong (1900–1971), jazz trumpeter, singer, and bandleader

Sidney Bechet (1897–1959), jazz saxophonist and clarinetist

Geoffrey Beene (b. 1927), fashion designer

Arna Bontemps (1902–1973), novelist and poet, member of Harlem Renaissance

Terry Bradshaw (b. 1948), professional football quarterback

Truman Capote (1924–1984), novelist, short-story writer, and creator, with *In Cold Blood,* of the "nonfiction novel"

Van Cliburn (b. 1934), classical pianist

Harry Connick, Jr. (b. 1967), singer and pianist

Michael De Bakey (b. 1908), pioneering heart surgeon

Ernest Gaines (b. 1933), novelist, author of *The Autobiography of Miss Jane Pittman*

Louis Moreau Gottschalk (1829–1869), pianist and composer

Shirley Ann Grau (b. 1929), novelist and short-story writer; winner of Pulitzer Prize for *The Hard Blue Sky* (1958)

Ernest Guiraud (1837–1892), composer

Lillian Hellman (1905–1984), playwright and memoirist

Clementine Hunter (1888–1986), folk artist

Mahalia Jackson (1911–1972), gospel singer

Dorothy Lamour (1914–1996), actress

Jerry Lee Lewis (b. 1935), pioneering rock 'n' roll singer and composer

Huey Long (1893-1935), Louisiana governor and U.S. senator

Ellis Marsalis (b. 1934), jazz musician, father of Wynton (b. 1961), Branford (b. 1960), and Delfeayo (b. 1965)

Jelly Roll Morton (Ferdinand Joseph Le Menthe) (1890–1941), jazz pianist, composer, and arranger

Aaron Neville (b. 1941), soul and rhythm & blues vocalist

Joe "King" Oliver (1885–1938), jazz cornetist

Edward "Kid" Ory (1886–1973), jazz trombonist and bandleader

Mel Ott (1909–1958), New York Giants player and manager

Anne Rice (b. 1941), novelist; also publishes as A. N. Roquelaure and Anne Rampling

Andrew Young (b. 1932), U.S. congressman, UN representative, and mayor of Atlanta

. . . and Great Places

Some interesting derivations of Louisiana place names.

Abbeville   Named for the Abbé Antoine Désiré Megret, who established a church here.

Algiers   Named in the 1830s after the North African city, then known chiefly for its pirates.

Aloha   Named after the Hawaiian greeting in the early 20th century, when Hawaiian songs were popular on the mainland.

Bogalusa   Choctaw for "black stream."

Brusly   Pronounced *BREW-lee*, the name comes from the practice of burning the brush to clear the land—*brulé* is French for "burned."

Calcasieu   French spelling of an Indian name meaning "crying eagle."

Catahoula   From the Choctaw, "beloved lake."

Cocodrie   American-French for "crocodile."

Gretna   An early justice of the peace performed marriages day or night, so the town was named after Gretna Green, a Scottish haven for runaway lovers.

Lecompte   Named (and misspelled) for a racehorse, Lecomte, that was raised on a plantation near Alexandria.

Mamou   Indian for "big hunting ground."

Monroe   Named not for the president but for a steamboat, the *James Monroe,* first steamboat on the Ouachita River (1819).

Natchitoches   Pronounced *NACK-i-tush,* it means "chestnut eaters" in a local Indian dialect.

Opelousas   From an Indian word meaning "black leg," with a French plural "s" tacked on.

Panola   Choctaw, "cotton."

Plaquemines   French spelling of Indian "plakemines," or "persimmons."

St. Amant   Named for the Amant family, pioneer settlers in that area of the state.

Slidell   Named after John Slidell, political boss of the state in the 1850s.

Transylvania   Once a busy lumber center, it is named not for the Central European region but for its literal Latin meaning, "beyond the forest."

Uneedus   The Lake Superior Piling Company in this farming village used the slogan "you need us," and the town adopted it.

Vacherie   French for "dairy farm" or "cattle ranch."

Westwego   Railroad cars passing through this town used to be marked in chalk with their direction. Most said "west we go."

Zwolle   Named by a Dutch immigrant, Jan De Goeijen, after his hometown in Holland.

Terrebonne   French for "good earth."

LOUISIANA BY THE SEASONS
A Perennial Calendar of Events and Festivals

Here is a selective listing of events that take place each year in the months noted; we suggest calling ahead to local chambers of commerce for dates and details.

January

Chalmette
Battle of New Orleans Celebration
Re-enactment at a National Historical Park.

Grand Chenier
Louisiana Fur and Wildlife Festival

New Orleans
Sugar Bowl
Top college football teams square off.

Shreveport
Mardi Gras in the Ark-La-Tex
Regional carnival celebration featuring parades, balls.

February

Acadiana
Courir de Mardi Gras
"The running of Mardi Gras" is held in several Cajun country towns.

Monroe
Black Heritage Parade

New Orleans
Mardi Gras
The most famous carnival of all, with 60-plus parades.

Winnfield
Krewe of the Kingfish Parade
Mardi Gras in the birthplace of Huey P. Long (the Kingfish).

Around the state
Mardi Gras celebrations. Dates vary year to year.

March

New Orleans
Tennessee Williams/New Orleans Literary Festival
Literary panels, theater productions, related events.

St. Francisville
Audubon Pilgrimage
Tours of Oakley House, where John James Audubon lived.

Vivian
Redbud Festival
Redbud trees in bloom.

Winnfield
Uncle Earl's Hog Dog Trials
Three-day festival features native Catahoula hunting dogs tracking wild hogs.

April

Angola
Arts and Crafts Festival
Features art created by inmates at Angola State Penitentiary.

Lafayette
Festival International de Louisiana

Marthaville
Louisiana State Fiddlers Championship

New Orleans
French Quarter Festival
Jazz, gospel, rhythm & blues, and food from Quarter restaurants.

Jazz and Heritage Festival
Two weekends of jazz with big-name musicians on 10 stages.

Oil City
Gusher Days

Shreveport
Holiday in Dixie
Ten-day festival commemorating the Louisiana Purchase.

Artbreak
Largest children's art festival in the state; juried exhibits.

May

Breaux Bridge
Crawfish Festival
Homage to the state crustacean: crawfish dinners, Cajun music, crafts.

Hemingbough
Louisiana Symphony Summerfest

Houma
St. Gregory Louisiana Praline Festival

Lake Charles
Contraband Days
A celebration of famed pirate Jean Lafitte.

Shreveport
Mudbug Madness
Four-day festival of Cajun
heritage and crawfish.

June

Bunkie
Louisiana Corn Festival

Lacombe
Bayou Lacombe Crab Festival

Natchitoches
*Melrose Plantation Arts and
Crafts Festival*
Two-day festival at historic
plantation that was home to
folk artist Clementine Hunter.

July

Des Allemands
Louisiana Catfish Festival

Farmerville
Louisiana Watermelon Festival

Grand Isle
International Tarpon Rodeo

Lake Charles
Cajun Music and Food Festival
Sponsored by the Cajun French
Music Association.
Natchitoches Folk Festival

August

Hammond
*Tangipahoa Black Heritage
Festival*

Lafayette
*Le Cajun Music Awards and
Festival*

Plaquemine
Gospel Fest

September

Kenner
St. Rosalie Procession
Sicilian community event; can-
dlelight procession and fireworks.

Morgan City
Shrimp and Petroleum Festival
Labor Day weekend celebration
in the erstwhile Jumbo Shrimp
Capital of the World.

New Iberia
*Louisiana Sugar Cane Festival
and Fair*

Plaisance
Zydeco Festival
Celebrated near Opelousas,
birthplace of zydeco music.

October

Crowley
International Rice Festival
Weekend festival in rice-growing
center.

Natchitoches
Natchitoches Pilgrimage
Tours of grand homes from
antebellum and later eras.

New Orleans
Art for Art's Sake
Warehouse District gallery tours.
Gathering of the Coven
Writer Anne Rice's Halloween
party; culminates in a gala
Coven Ball.

Opelousas
Louisiana Yambilee Festival
Homage to the noble yam.

St. Martinville
Pepper Festival

Shreveport
Louisiana State Fair

Zwolle
Zwolle Tamale Festival

November

Colfax
Louisiana Pecan Festival

Shreveport
Christmas in Roseland
Gardens of the American Rose
Center are transformed by
1 million Christmas lights.

Ville Platte
Louisiana Cajun Gumbo Festival

December

Garyville
Wheelbarrow Parade
LSU and Tulane University fans
bet on the "crosstown rival"
football game; losers push win-
ners in decorated floats along a
2-mile parade route.

Natchitoches
Christmas Festival of Lights
Lights are strung along the
downtown riverbank.

St. Martinville
Creole Holidays
In the Longfellow–Evangeline
State Commemorative Area.

St. Francisville
Christmas in the Country
Villagers dress in 1820s costume
for this three-day festival.

WHERE TO GO
Museums, Attractions, Gardens, and Other Arts Resources

Call for seasons and hours when open.

Museums

ALEXANDRIA MUSEUM OF ART
933 Main St., Alexandria, 318-443-3458

Centerpiece of Alexandria riverfront, with a strong collection of 20th-century Louisianian and Southern artists.

AMISTAD RESEARCH CENTER AT TULANE UNIVERSITY
6823 St. Charles Ave., New Orleans, 504-865-5535

World's largest collection on ethnic history and U.S. race relations; includes many artworks by African Americans.

BAYOU FOLK MUSEUM
Main St., Cloutierville, 318-379-2233

Home of writer Kate Chopin between 1879 and 1884; houses a collection of artifacts and antique furniture.

ARNA BONTEMPS AFRICAN-AMERICAN MUSEUM AND CULTURAL CENTER
1327 3rd St., Alexandria, 318-473-4692

The childhood home of Bontemps, a writer and member of the Harlem Renaissance, is now a museum.

THE CABILDO
701 Chartres St., New Orleans, 504-568-6958

The seat of Spanish Louisiana, the restored Cabildo contains historical exhibits.

CONTEMPORARY ARTS CENTER (CAC)
900 Camp St., New Orleans, 504-523-1216

A converted warehouse, this museum provides a showcase for innovative exhibits and musical presentations.

HISTORIC NEW ORLEANS COLLECTION
533 Royal St., New Orleans, 504-523-4662

Four historic French Quarter buildings housing historic records and a permanent exhibit of Louisiana history.

IMPERIAL CALCASIEU MUSEUM
204 W. Sallier, Lake Charles, 318-439-3797

Historical displays and re-creations, a fine arts gallery, and a library with a collection of Audubon prints.

INTERNATIONAL PETROLEUM MUSEUM & EXPOSITION
111 First St., Morgan City, 504-384-3744

Features "Mr. Charlie," grandfather of all transportable drilling rigs.

LOUISIANA CHILDREN'S MUSEUM
420 Julia St., New Orleans, 504-586-0725

Two floors of hands-on exhibits, including a math and science lab, plus a theater for live performances.

LSU MUSEUM OF ART
Memorial Tower, Louisiana State University, Baton Rouge, 504-388-4003

Works by Louisiana artists Caroline Durieux and Adrien Persac, and a large collection of locally crafted silver.

LSU RURAL LIFE MUSEUM
Exit 160 (Essen Lane) from I-10, Baton Rouge, 504-765-2437

Outdoor folk museum re-creates an antebellum plantation.

MEADOWS MUSEUM OF ART
2911 Centenary Blvd., Shreveport 318-869-5169

On the campus of Centenary College; features paintings of Southeast Asia by French artist Jean Despujols, as well as rotating exhibits.

NEW ORLEANS HISTORIC VOODOO MUSEUM
724 Dumaine St., New Orleans, 504-523-7685

Reputedly the world's only private museum devoted to voodoo, this small French Quarter building is packed with charms, potions, and some downright bizarre exhibits.

NEW ORLEANS MUSEUM OF ART (NOMA)
1 Collins Diboll Dr., City Park, New Orleans,
504-488-2631
*More than 35,000 works in a lovely neoclassical building
designed by Samuel Marx. Excellent collection of regional art.*

OGDEN MUSEUM OF SOUTHERN ART
615 Howard Ave., New Orleans, 504-539-9600
*Important collection of Louisiana and Southern regional art;
opens to the public in early 2000.*

THE PRESBYTERE
751 Chartres St., New Orleans, 504-568-6968
*Built in 1795 to house priests; now part of the Louisiana
State Museum complex; displays changing exhibits.*

OLD U.S. MINT
400 Esplanade Ave., New Orleans
*Erstwhile mint houses a splendid display of Mardi Gras
costumes and artifacts, and an excellent jazz collection.*

REBECCA'S DOLL MUSEUM
4500 Bon Aire Dr., Monroe, 318-343-5627
More than 2,000 dolls and furnishings.

W.H. TUPPER GENERAL MERCHANDISE MUSEUM
311 N. Main St., Jennings, 318-821-5532
*The entire inventory of a rural general store that closed in
the 1950s; many items in original boxes..*

Attractions

ACADIAN VILLAGE
West Broussard Rd., Lafayette, 318-981-2364
*Authentic structures from early 19th-century Acadiana,
restored and furnished with Cajun household items.*

AQUARIUM OF THE AMERICAS
1 Canal St., New Orleans, 504-581-6429
*Jellyfish, white alligators, the world's largest shark collec-
tion—7,500 aquatic specimens in all.*

BLAINE KERN'S MARDI GRAS WORLD
233 Newton St., New Orleans, 888-546-2734
*Vast workshop where Mardi Gras floats and costumes are
made. Tours daily.*

LAFAYETTE CEMETERY NO. 1
1428 Washington Ave., New Orleans
*One of the famed "cities of the dead," built above ground
because of the marshy terrain. Group tour.*

LOUISIANA STATE CAPITOL
State Capitol Dr., Baton Rouge, 504-342-7317
*Art Deco edifice built during Governor Huey Long's
administration; nation's tallest capitol.*

McILHENNY TABASCO FACTORY
Avery Island, 800-634-9599
*Factory tours and samples of the red-hot red sauce, made
and bottled on Avery Island.*

OLD STATE CAPITOL
North Blvd. at River Rd., Baton Rouge, 504-342-0500
*Built in the 1840s, the Gothic Revival castle now houses a
museum of the history of state government.*

POVERTY POINT
P.O. Box 276, Epps, 318-926-5492
*A collection of mysterious ridges and mounds created
between 1700 and 700 B.C.; largest earthworks in the
Western Hemisphere.*

ST. LOUIS CATHEDRAL BASILICA
Jackson Square, New Orleans, 504-525-9585
*The gift of a Spanish benefactor in 1794, it's the nation's
oldest active cathedral.*

VERMILIONVILLE
1600 Surrey St., Lafayette, 800-992-2968
*A 23-acre folk museum devoted to early Acadian and
Creole life in southern Louisiana.*

Homes and Gardens

AMERICAN ROSE CENTER
8877 Jefferson-Paige Rd., Shreveport, 318-938-5402
Largest rose garden in the U.S.: more than 40 acres of roses.

BEAUREGARD-KEYES HOUSE
1113 Chartres St., New Orleans, 504-523-7257
Greek Revival cottage built in 1826; home of General P. G. T. Beauregard and novelist Frances Parkinson Keyes.

HODGES GARDENS
P.O. Box 340, Florien, 800-354-3523
A pine forest retreat created in the 1940s, with seasonal displays of flowers and a 225-acre lake.

HOUMAS HOUSE
La. Rt. 942, just north of Burnside, 504-473-7841
Two linked houses—an 1840s mansion and an 18th-century Spanish-French building.

LAURA, A CREOLE PLANTATION
2247 La. Rt. 18, Vacherie, 504-265-7590
The slave quarters of this 1805 mansion are said to be the place where Joel Chandler Harris heard the tales he would turn into the "Br'er Rabbit" stories.

LIVE OAK GARDENS
Jefferson Island, 318-365-3332
Palatial home and 20 acres of gardens designed and built in 1870 by stage actor Joseph Jefferson.

LONGUE VUE
7 Bamboo Rd., New Orleans, 504-488-5488
Classic 45-room Greek Revival mansion, surrounded by eight acres of mansion.

LOUISIANA STATE ARBORETUM
Route 3, Box 494, Ville Platte, 318-363-6289
State's only preservation area, with outdoor exhibits, trails, guided tours, and labeled plant life.

ALEXANDRE MOUTON HOUSE
1122 Lafayette St., Lafayette, 318-234-2208
Built in 1800 by town founder Jean Mouton; houses a collection of his belongings and Mardi Gras costumes.

MADEWOOD PLANTATION
La. Rt. 308 near Napoleonville, 504-369-7151
Restored Palladian-style 1846 mansion created by New Orleans architect Henry Howard for the Pugh family and decorated with period antiques.

NOTTOWAY PLANTATION
P.O. Box 160, White Castle, 504-545-2730
Huge Italianate/Greek Revival building from 1859 boasted indoor plumbing, gas lighting, and coal fireplaces ahead of its time. Tours; accommodations.

OAK ALLEY PLANTATION
3 miles west of Vacherie on La. Rt. 18, 504-265-2151
The restored rooms are beautiful, but the main attraction is the splendid oak allée leading to the Mississippi River.

SHADOWS-ON-THE-TECHE
317 East Main St., New Iberia, 318-369-6446
Restored 1834 plantation house bequeathed to the National Trust for Historic Preservation.

Other Resources

LOUISIANA OFFICE OF TOURISM
P.O. Box 94291, Baton Rouge, 800-334-8626

LOUISIANA OFFICE OF STATE PARKS
DEPT. OF CULTURE, RECREATION AND TOURISM
P.O. Drawer 1111, Baton Rouge, 504-342-8111

NATIONAL FOREST INFORMATION
KISATCHIE NATIONAL FOREST
P.O. Box 5500, Pineville, 318-473-7160

CREDITS

The authors have made every effort to reach copyright holders of text and owners of illustrations, and wish to thank those individuals and institutions that permitted the reprinting of text or the reproduction of works in their collections. Those credits not listed in the captions are provided below; References are to page numbers; the designations *a, b,* and *c* indicate position of illustrations on pages.

Text

Bourne Co. Music Publishers: "Every Man a King" by Huey P. Long and Castro Carazo. Copyright © 1935 by Bourne Co. Copyright renewed. All rights reserved. International copyright secured. ASCAP.

Farrar, Straus, Giroux, Inc.: Excerpt from *The Cajuns: From Acadia to Louisiana* by William Faulkner Rushton. Copyright © 1979. By permission of Farrar, Straus, Giroux, Inc.

HarperCollins Publishers, Inc.: Oysters Rockefeller recipe from *The New York Times Cookbook* by Craig Claiborne. Copyright © 1990. Reprinted by permission of HarperCollins Publishers, Inc.

JCA Literary Agency: From *The Hard Blue Sky* by Shirley Ann Grau. Copyright © 1958 by Alfred A. Knopf, Inc. By permission of the JCA Literary Agency.

Little, Brown & Co., Inc.: Excerpt from *The Indians of Louisiana* by Fred Kniffen. Copyright © 1945. Reprinted by permission of Little, Brown & Co., Inc.

Lord John Press: From *The City of the Dead* by Walker Percy. Copyright © 1984 by Lord John Press.

Louisiana State University Press: From the foreword by Andrei Codrescu in *Elysium: A Gathering of Souls* by Sandra Russell Clark. Copyright © 1997. Excerpt from "The Storm," from *The Awakening: Selected Stories* by Kate Chopin. Copyright © 1986. Reprinted by permission of LSU Press.

New Directions Publishing Corporation: by Tennessee Williams, from *A Streetcar Named Desire.* Copyright © 1947 by Tennessee Williams. Reprinted by permission of New Directions Publishing Corp.

Pelican Publishing, Inc.: Two excerpts from *Gumbo Ya-Ya* by Lyle Saxon. Copyright © 1987. Excerpt from *Fabulous*

New Orleans by Lyle Saxon. Copyright © 1928. Used by permission of the publisher: Pelican Publishing, Inc.

Penguin Putnam Inc.: From *Southerners* by Marshall Frady. Copyright © 1980 by Marshall Frady. Used by permission of Dutton Signet, a division of Penguin Putnam Inc.

Random House, Inc.: Excerpt from *Selected Poems, New and Old, 1923–1975* by Robert Penn Warren. Copyright © 1966.

St. Martin's Press, Inc.: From *New Orleans Mourning.* Copyright © 1990 by Julie Smith. Reprinted by permission of St. Martin's Press, Inc.

Warner-Chappell, Inc.: Excerpt from the song "Louisiana 1927," by Randy Newman. Reprinted by permission of Warner-Chappell, Inc.

Illustrations

JAY P. ALTMAYER COLLECTION, MOBILE, AL: **68** *Poker Game on a Riverboat.* Oil on cardboard. 7 x 10"; CORBIS: **13b&c** Philip Gould; **20; 50, 55b, 60a, 74b, 87b** Robert Holmes, **89** Philip Gould; FRED BENTON COLLECTION: **53**; SHARON DINKINS COLLECTION: **45b** THE GAINES FAMILY: **74a**; ELLIN AND BARON GORDON: **84a** *Seven-Headed Dragon/Monster.* Paint on sheet iron. 23¼ x 28 x 1¾"; WILLIAM GUION: **23a, 87c** HISTORIC NEW ORLEANS COLLECTION: **5** *The End of an Era.* Photo print. 11 x 14"; **16** *Duc D'Orleans.* Lithograph. 6½ x 4¼"; **29b** *Taking Possession of Louisiana and the River Mississippi.* Color lithograph. 18 x 25"; **32a** Ensign, **32b** *The Louisiana Purchase and American Expansion.* Hand-colored engraving. 27¾ x 21⅜"; **33** *Battle of New Orleans.* Oil on canvas. 18¼ x 24½"; **39a** *A Plantation Burial.* Oil on canvas. 52¾ x 81½"; **41** *Port and City of New Orleans.* Oil on canvas. 9 x 13"; **54b, 65b, 67a** *Woodward House, Lowerline and Benjamin Streets.* Oil on canvas. 24⅛ x 29⅜"; **76a** *French Opera House.* 16 x 23½"; RON KIMBALL: **15a**; LOUISIANA STATE MUSEUM, NEW ORLEANS: **11** Chamber of Commerce Chair. Solid oak. 85 x 32½ x 28"; **19** *Long Billed Curlew.* Oil on canvas. 16 x 24"; **28b** *Père Antoine.* Oil on canvas. 101¾ x 65¾". Lent by the Archdiocese of New Orleans to Louisiana State Museum; **29a** *Marianne Celeste Dragon.* Oil on canvas. 37¼ x 30¼"; **31** *Evangeline.* Oil on canvas. 80 x 83"; **60b** Presentation chalice. Silver. 6 ½ x 4"; **61b** Louisiana-crafted table; **72a** Gauntlet. **76b** Cover of a libretto; LOUISIANA

STATE UNIVERSITY MUSEUM OF ART, BATON ROUGE: **9** *Cafe Tupinamba.* Oil on canvas. 32 x 40". Gift of Charles Phelps Manship, Jr. in memory of his parents, Leora and Charles P. Manship, Sr.; **34a** *The Battle of Port Hudson.* Oil on canvas. 30 x 40". Gift of the friends of the LSU Museum of Art; MR. AND MRS. KEITH C. MARSHALL COLLECTION, NEW ORLEANS: **56** *The Shooting of Huey Long.* Multistage on canvas. 40 x 30"; LE MIEUX GALLERIES, NEW ORLEANS: **75b** *Portrait of Tennessee Williams.* Oil on wood. 22 x 36"; **82b** *Mourning Shadows.* Oil on canvas. 26 x 26"; LOUISIANA STATE EXHIBIT MUSEUM: **26a&b**; MUSÉE DES BEAUX-ARTS, PARIS/ART RESOURCE, NY: **37** *Inside the New Orleans Cotton Office.* Oil on canvas. 28¾ x 36¼". Photo Erich Lessing; MUSEUM OF THE CONFEDERACY: **34b** Flag; **35a**; NATIONAL GEOGRAPHIC IMAGE COLLECTION: **12a** Louisiana flag. Illustration by Marilyn Dye Smith; **12b** Pelican and magnolia. Illustration by Robert E. Hynes; NEW ORLEANS HISTORIC VOODOO MUSEUM: **51a** *Portrait of Marie Laveau.* Oil on canvas. 24 x 38"; **87a** Voodoo doll; NEW ORLEANS MUSEUM OF ART: **13a** *Spirit of Louisiana.* Oil on canvas. 45 x 27"; **27a** *Indians Walking Along a Bayou.* Oil on canvas. 24 x 40". Gift of William E. Groves; **30a** *Portrait of a Free Woman of Color.* Oil on canvas. 38¾ x 31". Gift of Felix H. Kuntz; **42a** *Blue Crab and Terrapins.* Gouache on cardboard. 24¾ x 15½". Gift of the Estate of Samuel W. Weis; **46** *Second Ursulines Convent and Priest's House.* Oil crayon on cardboard. 22 x 28". Gift of Edgar Stern Family Fund; **47a** *Her First Communion.* Oil on canvas. 39 x 24". Gift of Mr. and Mrs. Richard B. Kaufmann in honor of E. John Bullard; **48** *Permanent Address.* Oil on board. 30 x 32". The T. Jeff and Lillian G. Feibleman Collection; **67b** *Portrait of William Woodward.* Oil on canvas. 27½ x 19½". Gift of Mr. Carl E. Woodward; NEW YORK CITY PUBLIC LIBRARY, OFFICE OF SPECIAL COLLECTIONS: **36a** *Wild Indigo; Doggwood Tree.* Astor, Lenox, & Tilden Foundation; ROGER HOUSTON OGDEN COLLECTION: **22** *A Southern Stream.* Oil on canvas. 22 x 16"; OGDEN MUSEUM OF SOUTHERN ART, UNIVERSITY OF NEW ORLEANS: **2** *Cypress Point, Bayou Lacombe, Louisiana.* Oil on canvas. 20 x 24"; **18** *Bayou Plaquemines.* Oil on canvas. 20½ x 36"; **21** *Tangled in Deep.* Oil on canvas. 43½ x 79½"; **25** *Ship Natchez of New Orleans.* Oil on canvas. 28¼ x 36"; **35** *Louisiana Tigers.* Wood with carved bone overlay. 4 x 9½ x 6½"; **43** *The Blessing of the Shrimp Fleet.* Oil on canvas. 21¼ x 26¼"; **45a** *Avery Island Salt Mines.* Oil on canvas. 23 x 30½"; **47b** *Baptism on Cane River.* Oil on window shade. 36 x 72"; **52** *Violet Locks.* Oil on canvas. 27 x 39"; **54a** *French Quarter Scene.* Oil on canvas. 15 x 18"; **57a** *Huey and President Smith.* Black-and-white print. 20 x 16"; **59a** *Maison Pontchartrain.* Oil on panel. 11½ x 9¼"; **66a** *Iris Field Near Newcomb Green House.* Watercolor on paper. 19½ x 13½"; **66b** *Newcomb Vase with Magnolias.* Ceramic. 9½ x 7", *Newcomb Vase with Palm and Moon.* Ceramic. 14 x 6"; **69** *New Orleans Ladies.* Gouache on paper. 16 x 20"; **70a** Invitation to a ball.; **70b** Sketch for Mardi Gras float. 16 x 20"; PANORAMIC IMAGES: **14a**; PEABODY MUSEUM, HARVARD UNIVERSITY: **27b** Etched pot; REED/WILLIAMS: **15a**; GEORGE RODRIGUE LIBRARY, LAFAYETTE, LA: **30b** *Playing Bourré.* Oil on canvas. 30 x 40"; **84b** *Novena for the Oaks.* Oil on linen. 36 x 48"; ARTHUR ROGER GALLERY, NEW ORLEANS: **1** *Washboard Player.* Oil on canvas. 60 x 40"; **82a** *Pond View.* Acrylic on masonite. 11½ x 21½"; **83a** *Treasures.* Oil on panel 20 x 16"; **83b** *Figurative Wall Object.* Monotype on wood. 30 x 7 x 1"; **85a** *Composition 94-1.* Oil on canvas. 36 x 48"; STATE OF LOUISIANA: **12c** State seal; TULANE UNIVERSITY LIBRARY: **78a**; UNIVERSITY OF NORTH TEXAS PRESS: **23b** *Trumpet Creeper* from *American Wildflower Florilegium* by Jean Andrews; UPI/CORBIS-BETTMANN: **24, 79a**; THE WARNER COLLECTION OF GULF STATES PAPER CORPORATION, TUSCALOOSA, AL: **36b** *Comin' from the Market near Baton Rouge.* Oil on canvas. 13½ x 23½"; NATALIE WINANS: **38a** *Rice Festival, Crowley.* Black-and-white print; YA/YA: **85b** Chair by Chris Peratore. 12 x 14 x 28"

Acknowledgments

Walking Stick Press wishes to thank our project staff: Miriam Lewis, Joanna Lynch, Kina Sullivan, Thérèse Martin, Laurie Donaldson, Lani Gallegos, Nancy Barnes, and Adam Ling. For other assistance with *Louisiana,* we are especially grateful to: Laurel Anderson/Photosynthesis, Lindsay Kefauver/Visual Resources, H. Parrot Bacot of Louisiana State University, Kenneth W. Barnes of the Ogden Collection, Charlie Byrd of the Louisiana Tourism Office, Sharon Glasheen of the Louisiana State Museum; Jennifer Ickes of the New Orleans Museum of Art, John Magill of the Historic New Orleans Collection, and photographers Syndey Byrd, William Guion, and Richard Sexton.